*The
Strawberry
Statement*

The Strawberry Statement— Notes of a College Revolutionary
by James Simon Kunen

WILEY-BLACKWELL

A John Wiley & Sons, Ltd., Publication

This edition first published 1968
© 1968, 1969, 1995 James S. Kunen

Edition history; First published 1968 by Random House
First printed by Wiley-Blackwell 2008
Blackwell Publishing was acquired by John Wiley & Sons in February 2007. Blackwell's publishing
program has been merged with Wiley's global Scientific, Technical, and Medical business to form
Wiley-Blackwell.

Registered Office
John Wiley & Sons Ltd, The Atrium, Southern Gate, Chichester, West Sussex, PO19 8SQ, United
Kingdom

Editorial Offices
350 Main Street, Malden, MA 02148-5020, USA
9600 Garsington Road, Oxford, OX4 2DQ, UK
The Atrium, Southern Gate, Chichester, West Sussex, PO19 8SQ, UK

For details of our global editorial offices, for customer services, and for information about how to apply
for permission to reuse the copyright material in this book please see our website at
www.wiley.com/wiley-blackwell.

ISBN 978-1-8810-8-9520

A catalogue record for this book is available from the British Library.

3   2009

Cover art by Paula Shields, 1973

*To my distinguished colleagues,
associates in the field,
revolutionary cohorts, parents,
siblings, my friends and my
enemies, everyone I've known
and everyone I've yet to meet, and
especially everybody else*

The world feels hurt
'Cause of the wars.

The world feels ashamed
'Cause of the wars.

The people don't feel
What the world feels like.

Jill Rittmaster, Grade four
The Town School, New York City, 1968

I could really see going crazy.

Casey

To the cops, we're all niggers.

Lower East Side organizer (white)

Sometimes I feel like such an incredible nothing.

Anonymous

Contents

Author's Preface to the Brandywine Press Edition

"You've got the power," I wrote in *The Strawberry Statement* 27 years ago. "You make millions of people suffer . . . Well cut it out, will you? Just stop it. If you won't stop it we'll stop you." The "we" I was presuming to speak for were the student protesters of the '60s, and the "you" were the remote and powerful men who were exploiting and oppressing "The People." Three decades later, it's terribly clear that my generation hasn't changed the world very much. The question is, how much has the world changed us?

As young "radicals," we considered ourselves the conscience of the nation. To us, the Vietnam War was a moral offense, not a question of politics; and we reacted to it in primarily moral, rather than political, terms. Somehow, by the strength of our youth, the nation would be wrenched from the grip of death, cleansed, made new. A "movement" without politics or program, we were defined largely by our shared lives on the campus—

millions of us getting stoned and listening to the Beatles—and by our opposition to the war. Now that war is long over, and we inhabit private worlds.

Still, when I speak with my old "radical" friends—none of whom are leading noticeably radical lives—I find that our basic values haven't changed that much. We're dismayed by the country's swing to the right and appalled by slashes in social programs. Why then aren't we heard from? Why aren't we marching in the streets?

Paradoxically, we felt a more excruciating responsibility for the acts of our nation as 18-year-olds who couldn't even vote than we do now. We took things more personally. We felt that *we* were bombing Vietnam, and *we* were allowing the less well-connected of our generation to die there. Now, we say, it's those Republicans who have declared all-out war on the poor and the powerless.

We no longer believe that we can remake the world. Instead we adapt to it and act cautiously, because we have much more to lose. We have our *careers*. In the booming economy of the '60s, the affluent youth's greatest concern about a career was how to avoid one. A career was part of the System, within which success and exploitation, work and war, were inextricably linked. ("Work! Study! Get ahead! Kill!" we used to chant at demonstrations.) Also, embarking on a career meant accepting the constraints of adulthood. I thought if I didn't settle down, I could stay young forever. I was wrong. You get old whether you're wearing a necktie or not.

When I was a "kid"—a word we applied to ourselves well into our twenties—I avowed a profound aversion to wealth. All I wanted, I used to say, was to raise a family in a decent home and be able to spend a few weeks at the beach. That's all I want now, but I find that these modest ends require massive means. It's hard to renounce materialism when materialism is renouncing you.

Our middle-class instinct (subliminal, unshakable) to "make something of yourself" and contribute to society, has led almost all of us down the Establishment road—what we used to call selling out. We like to think that our careers give us more effective ways to act on our values than we had as students. We try to do good and do well at the same time.

Meanwhile, people sleep on the streets. We know we really ought to find the time and the courage to do something about it. (Things to do today: call insurance broker, add to IRA, smash the state.)

At least we have a past to live up to. We helped end one war, and the continuing effect of our action restrains our country from getting into new ones. It's good that there was a time when we stood up for what we believed in—which, as you get along and go along, is not something you do every day.

James S. Kunen
Brooklyn, N.Y.
June 1995

*The
Strawberry
Statement*

Intro 1
About the Book

My question is a simple one: who am I to write a book? I don't know. I'm just writing it. You're just reading it. Let's not worry about it.

Intro 2
Who Wrote the Book

I wrote the Book.

I should like to point out immediately that just because I happened to be born in 1948, it doesn't mean that what I have to say as a nineteen-year-old is worth any more than what nineteen-year-olds had to say in, to pick a year at random, 1920. To say that youth is what's happening is absurd. It's always been happening. Everyone is nineteen, only at different times. This youth-cult scene is a disservice to everyone. I'm anticipating a severe psychological set-back when I turn twenty, and I don't know what I'm going to do when my youth-fare card runs out. As for this "don't-trust-anyone-over-30" shit, I agree in principle, but I think they ought to drop the zero.

What sort of man gets busted at Columbia? I don't know. I got busted at Columbia and I, for one, strongly support trees (and, in the larger sense, forests), flowers, mountains and hills, also valleys, the ocean, wiliness (when used for good), good, little children, people, tremendous record-setting snowstorms, hurricanes, swimming underwater, nice policemen, unicorns, extra-inning ball games up to twelve innings, pneumatic jackhammers (when they're not too close), the dunes in North Truro on Cape Cod, liberalized abortion laws, and Raggedy Ann dolls, among other things.

I do not like Texas, people who go to the zoo to be arty, the Defense Department, the name "Defense Department," the fly buzzing around me as I write this, protective tariffs, little snowstorms that turn to slush, the short days of winter, extra-inning ball games over twelve innings, calling people consumers, pneumatic jackhammers immediately next to the window, and G.I. Joe dolls. Also racism, poverty and war. The latter three I'm trying to do something about.

But I am not a nihilist. I do like some things.

I should add that I have never been able to stand at a high place without thinking about jumping off.

Intro 3
Who We Are

People want to know who we are, and some think they know who we are. Some think we're a bunch of snot-nosed brats. It's difficult to say really who we are. We don't have snot on our noses.

What we do have is hopes and fears, or ups and downs, as they are called.

A lot of the time we are very unhappy, and we try to cheer ourselves up by thinking. We think how lucky we are to be able to go to school, to have nice clothes and fine things and to eat well and have money and be healthy. How lucky we are really. But we remain unhappy. Then we attack ourselves for self-pity, and become more unhappy, and still more unhappy over being sad.

We're unhappy because of the war, and because of poverty and the hopelessness of politics, but also because we sometimes get put down by girls or boys, as the case may be, or feel lonely and alone and lost.

And who we are is people in New York City.

New York is the most exciting city in the world, and also the cruddiest place to be that I can conceive of. The city, where when you see someone on the subway you know you will never see him again. The city, where the streets are dead with the movement of people brushing by, like silt in a now-dry riverbed, stirred by the rush of a dirty wind. The city, where you walk along on the hard floor of a giant maze with walls much taller than people and full of them. The city is an island and feels that way; not enough room, very separate. You have to walk on right-angle routes, can't see where you're going to, only where you are, can only see a narrow part of sky, and never any stars. It's a giant maze you have to fight through, like a rat, but unlike the rat you have no reward awaiting you at the end. There is no end, and you don't know what you're supposed to be looking for.

And unlike the rat, you are not alone. You are instead lonely. There is loneliness as can exist only in the midst of numbers and numbers of people who don't know you, who don't care about you, who won't let you care about them.

Everywhere you walk you hear a click-clack. The click-clack of your walking never leaves you, reminding you all the time that you are at the bottom of a box. The earth is trapped beneath concrete and tar and you are locked away from it. Nothing grows.

All of this makes us sad. And all of this is at Columbia, is Columbia, for Columbia is New York. Leaving the school or its city really doesn't help. Once you live in New York you are locked in the city, and the city is locked in you.

On the beach or in the woods the click-clack follows you, and you carry pavement beneath your feet. The walls are all around, for you have lived with people and away from them. You know the story on the world; you see how far people are. And you feel quite sad.

But sadness is not despair so long as you can get angry. And we have become angry at Columbia. Not having despaired, we are able to see things that need to be fought, and we fight. We have fought, we are fighting, we will fight.

Intro 4
How the Book Was Written

Writing a book is a lot like having a baby; they both involve bringing something into the world that wasn't there before, and they're both a pain in the ass.

This book was written on napkins and cigarette packs and hitchhiking signs. It was spread all over, but so is my mind. I exhibit a marked tendency to forget things. I can remember only three things at a time. If I think of a fourth thing, I forget the first. Like a cigarette machine. You take one pack out—all the rest fall down a notch. Exactly analogous in every salient detail.

The best, truest way to read this book would be to rip it up and throw the scraps all over your house. Then, later, should you come across a piece, read it, or don't read it, depending upon how you feel. Or, better, save it until four o'clock in the morning when you would rather do almost anything else, and read it then.

Above all, don't spend too much time reading it because I didn't spend much time writing it.

You will notice that a great deal of this book simply relates little things I've done and thought. It may seem completely irrelevant to Columbia. That's the way it goes.

Before the Shit Hit the Fan at Columbia

I existed before. I passed through quite a bit of time, and I took notes, to help me differentiate one day from another. Here come some of them now. They may help you to figure out where I'm at, as we youths say.

WAY BEFORE

In the summer following high school I made the "let's-see-how-tough-you-are-kid" scene at a place called Outward Bound in Oregon.

Monday, August 15, 1966: All my life "glacier," "crevasse," "moraine," etc., have just been words in a book. Today I actually climbed all over them. Hot shit.

Tuesday, August 16, 1966: Up at 5:30 A.M. to climb mountain on a breakfast of tea and honey. No exultation at reaching peak; if you decided to turn around ten yards short of the top I'd consider it a twenty-yard shortcut and fine with me. Airplane-like

10,000 foot perspective is mildly amusing, but not sufficiently so to keep me from falling asleep.

Then I became a college student.

Tuesday, October 25, 1966, 4:00 A.M. I have just finished my Contemporary Civilization paper on "The Abbot of Benedict's *Regula* vs. Plato's Philosopher King." Five and a half hours producing a mammoth compost heap, a putrid dung-mound.

Saturday, October 29, 1966: I must answer that yes, I did have some lonely moments at college, if I'm ever asked.

Thursday, December 15, 1966: Just heard that Walt Disney died. I remember a conversation with my brother a long time ago when we were thinking little. He said when Walt Disney died he'd be called "the man who made America happy." Now we'll see.

People will joke that his last movie was so bad that the reviews killed him. Probably he just died, though. At sixty-five, "and the world mourns." Of course it doesn't really, but it at least notices, which is certainly some tribute. That would have been a comfort to Walt, as he lay dying. Of course, if he just dropped dead, then it wouldn't have been a comfort to him.

Sunday, March 19, 1967, 10:18–10:20 P.M. I think I would like to be—when I am something—the Pope, or an international sex symbol, or both; Chancellor of the Exchequer, Viscount General, or a reindeer magnate and parking-meter racket boss, or a kingpin or gigolo and itinerant librarian, or perhaps a cowboy on the pampas or a gaucho or tundra inhabitant who lives elsewhere to be near the surf. (Unless, of course, I get the opportunity to be a W.W. II U-boat captain.)

No, I have no statement to make at this time, except I'm still on the waiting list in a lot of ways.

Sunday, May 7, 1967: I'm still on the waiting list in a lot of ways. I'm waiting to get back into the first boat at crew. Being taken

out was cruel and upsetting. Sometimes I loved crew and sometimes I hated it, but I gave myself to it, and when you give yourself to something you don't want to be spit out.

My friend the bowman and I figured out that, on the basis of
the three dollars lunch money we're given for rowing a seven-
minute race, we're earning $57,000 a year, plus prize money and
advertising royalties, for our rowing efforts. We row seven miles a
day, come freezing rain, snow, a blood-red moon, or what may.
It's a living. (In a year you spend approximately 700 hours pre-
paring for a season of races which take an aggregate of about
forty-five minutes to row.)

Tuesday, May 30, 1967: I've been wanting to talk to somebody
important about the war, and tonight, after a month, I finally got
through on the phone to Ambassador Bunker in Saigon. I told
him I thought he was an ambassador from a U.S. government to
a U.S. government. He couldn't go along with me on that, but
he did say he'd write me a letter explaining what he was about. He
admitted that he hadn't been on the streets to meet the people.

Wednesday, June 7, 1967: Received a seemingly personal letter
from the Bunk. He enclosed a copy of the South Vietnamese
Constitution, untranslated, in the original English. I noted that
it guaranteed the vote and free speech to everybody, except Communists and neutralists.

Tuesday, Wednesday, October 3, 4, 1967: Being from Massachu-
setts, naturally I was at both Red Sox–Minnesota games for
the pennant. The BoSox won. I was so afraid they wouldn't. How
could they? During the second game, they got behind. Third,
fourth inning, still behind. I prayed during that game. I put my
head in my hands and screamed to God: Okay, I recognize your
existence. Please, please, oh God, please let them win. What's
it to you? Why not let them win? Once, just once, let some small
thing come out right. Okay, so the owner might have been a
bigot once. Environment. What else could he be? He's not any

more. I listed all the reasons I could think of why Boston should win, not Minnesota. And we won. So happy.

NOT LONG BEFORE

My friends and I became preoccupied with the common nostalgic assertion that "these are the best years of your lives." We could accept the fact that the college years are exhausting, confusing, boring, troubled, frustrating and meaningless—that we could take in stride; we'd seen hard times before. But that everything subsequent would be worse was a concept difficult to grasp and, once grasped, impossible to accept.

So we took adaptive measures, which consisted chiefly of constructing an alternate world-structure in which we felt a bit more comfortable. It was a world rife with dangers, but the forces active in it were clearly enough defined to be successfully dealt with by anyone with the exquisite moral, physical, mental and philosophical finesse which we all possessed in it. Actually, even we used to lose more often then we'd win, but at least the legions of evil bothered to attack us. Naturally this sort of life allowed very little time for classes, and it required a hell of a lot of sleep.

A friend constantly called me up to confide that he had discovered various new aspects of a plot. The ring ring's phone plot, for instance. A quick look at an area-code map shows that the assignment of area codes follows no discernible pattern at all. Why? And the phone numbers of nearly everyone we knew were divisible by three.

The plots of Them, in fact, became so incomprehensibly multifarious that it seemed the only way to avoid them was never to leave your room or, ideally, your bed. But that might be playing right into Their hands.

In all my adventures I saw Them only once. They were standing on top of the Pentagon, looking at us through binoculars. I have a feeling it was not the only time They have seen me.

After about four months, understandably, dealing with Them became so tiresome that the whole endeavor moved from the

"Mildly Amusing" column into the "Pain in the Ass" column. (My roommate classifies everything into one of these two categories.)

The elite force counterposed to all of this evil was The Blue Berets. My friend Bill and I found ourselves in this corps when, at Andover (a prep school to which we went), we were faced with the challenge of swimming fifty yards underwater in order to get our lifesaving cards. Bill, glancing at the color of the water, remarked that we were going for our blue berets. The definition and function of our membership in this secret corps quickly spread well beyond the aquatic.

Bill was once taken ill, and came to me for an explanation of how this could possibly befall him. I reasoned that he was not sick, but thought he was sick. The immense power of a Blue Beret's thoughts pitted against the unimpeachable health of his body might produce an inner turmoil which would resemble "sickness."

A friend once asked me if a Blue Beret could get high. "If he wants to," I answered.

Other questions were more difficult. Could a Blue Beret give a karate chop so powerful as to break his own hand?

I never did arrive at an answer for that one, but it really doesn't matter, since I was "expunged from the rolls of the honored ones" some time ago for failure to quit smoking and a general lack of interest.

Floundering about in the rubble of my fantasy structure I latched onto The Letter. Every day I checked my mailbox, hoping to find "The Big Letter I've been waiting for." I wasn't sure what it would be, except that it would be a directive or executive order from my superior telling me to do something.

On January 17, 1968, I received, from Bill, a letter about The Letter.

Dear Jeem,

I'm using this guy's typewriter now and listening to his fine stereo tape recorder but we just don't get along at all because he keeps calling me a loser because he's a little hippie type who's sort of skinny and he's got this defensive-aggressive thing that he's got to get out. Whew, got that off my little ego-mind.

Try to understand about The Letter. I just wanted you to know that it will come, it is coming, it's on the way! Just don't give up hope, Jim, it could be in the mail now, or maybe some guy sitting in the hellhole in Khe Sanh has just written it to you and it might take a long time for it to get through or maybe she's writing it on her thigh off a Bermudian beach or LBJ is about to send you The Memo or God himself, the Great Nazz, is about to write it with the finger of God and inscribe it indelibly in the sacred corner the holy of holies of your heart but nor sleet nor rain nor gloom of night IT'S COMING. IT'S ON THE WAY.

This is a broken typewriter, well, throw a white ball against a dirty wall and it comes back dirty every time.

On February 20 I received a postcard, this one from another friend, Casey. "Dear Jim," I read. "The weather has been fine. We have had some snow. I feel good. Wish you all could come up for the big game on Saturday.—Rich." This, however, was written on a surface of white enamel, beneath which was hidden the true communication: "Down but not yet out.—C."

A good card, but The Letter will be a letter.

More recently, I received a letter from Rock, which concluded, "This letter is not—I repeat, is not—a transatlantic jetliner."

It was also not The Letter.

Expounding upon this sort of subject earned me the reputation of being crazy. I can remember feeling distinctly pleased at this. After I broke the toilet, however, people began to use the word "insane," which made me feel bad. I did suspect myself of enjoying feeling bad; but I felt bad nonetheless.

I broke the toilet with a Coke (reg.) bottle. I was trying to break the Coke bottle; the toilet was the first rigid object I saw; and it seems that glass breaks porcelain. Things went more predictably when I punched the lamp.

I had the hugest sophomore slump you can imagine. And I

finally just gave up and went around smashing things. Or I thought that I had given up. My brother said the punching and breaking were signs that I had not given up, that I was fighting, even if I couldn't see what to fight. On the other hand, maybe my brother was wrong and I had given up.

April 1, 1968: Johnson's Little Drama: Maybe it's an April fool. Or maybe he'll run as a Republican. (He said he wouldn't seek *his* party's nomination.) Or maybe he won't run because he'll suspend the elections. Or, most likely, he's playing for a draft, although if he got it people would say oh God and not vote for him.

I want to do something and know something. Yes, this is really a big thing in me. Think of all the feelings. I feel sorry for Johnson (that is, I feel sorry for what was presented on the screen, for what elicited sympathy) and I am hopeful for McCarthy and excited and confused and all the while completely alone in the room here. And worse, just for a second, the feeling that maybe I don't want the war to end, because then what will I do, then what will I hate?

Thursday, April 4, 1968: I was going to work for Martin Luther King's poor people's march, but now he's dead. I suppose there'll be one anyway. Anyway is the way things always end up going these days.

Then Rudd did the thing at the King Memorial Service. I wasn't there because we had double crew practice to take advantage of the suspension of classes. But there was a memorial service on campus, and President Kirk attended, and pious phrases were uttered honoring the memory of what the powerful choose to remember of Dr. King. And Rudd got up, in the middle of the service, and called the memorial service an obscenity, which it was, because, as he explained, while President Kirk was in there "honoring" Dr. King, his university was paying black maids less than they could collect on welfare, and insistently refusing collective bargaining and obstructing unionization of its kitchen workers, not to mention continuing the expansion policies which had in ten years almost completely expunged non-whites from Morningside Heights. Also, President Kirk's university was helping to form imperialist policy and prosecute the imperialist war that Dr. King opposed. President Kirk's little religious service was obscenely hypocritical, it was filthy. Rudd walked out. He was followed by many people. Soon he would be followed by many more.

CAST OF CHARACTERS

Grayson Kirk—President of Columbia University in the City of New York through August of 1968. An Eastern, scholarly Lyndon Johnson. Reputed to be arbitrary, tyrannical, out of touch with the people of his domain. Not known by students, but disliked all the same. Used to be professor of government a long time ago. Head of Security Section, Division of Political Studies, United States Department of State 1942–43.

Decorations: Commander in the Order of Orange-Nassau (Netherlands), 1952; Honorary Knight Commander of the Most Excellent Order of the British Empire, 1955; Commander in the French National Order of the Legion of Honor, 1956; Grande Ufficialato dell'Ordine al Merito della Republica (Italy), 1956; Associate Knight–The Grand Priory in the British Realm of the Most Venerable Order of the Hospital of St. John of Jerusalem, 1959; Medal of the Order of Taj (Iran), 1961; The Cross of the Grand Officer of the Order of George I (Greece), 1965; Order of the Sacred Treasure, First Class (Japan), 1965; Commandeur de l'Ordre des Palmes Académiques (France), 1966.

Director: American Council on Education (Commission on International Education); Belgian American Educational Foundation, Inc.; Consolidated Edison Company of New York; Council on Foreign Relations (President); Division

David B. Truman—Vice-President of Columbia University. Referred to as "Dean Truman" by everybody because he was, through 1967, Dean of Columbia College. Also used to be professor of government. Parallel to Hubert Humphrey: liberal reputation, friend of the little man (here, the student), very popular before he took V.P. office. Then trapped by loyalty to his superior and his job. Either that or exposed for a typical phony liberal.

Mark Rudd—President Columbia chapter Students for a Democratic Society. Junior in the college. Known to everyone, well known to few (the usual). Hardly revered, but certainly listened to.

Students for a Democratic Society—Just that. Defies more specific definition. Mixed bag. Activist, but often hampered by internal dissension. Maybe four hundred members; no one, least of all SDS, knows exactly. Meetings open, anyway. Influential in student life. Called "pukes" by the jocks.

Students Opposing SDS—Never could get their shit together: Students for a Free Campus, Students for Columbia University, Students for the Defense of Property Rights, Majority Coalition. All powerless because totally disorganized. Called "jocks" by the pukes.

IDA—Institute for Defense Analysis. Consortium of twelve universities doing research for the Pentagon. Columbia secretly, or at least very quietly, affiliated. Total contracts rather meager compared to many of Columbia's other war efforts. Chosen as a symbol for all university involvement with the war machine.

The Gym—An eleven-story private building to be built on public land, Morningside Park, which separates Columbia from Harlem. The community (blacks) could use a certain section of it at certain times, through a certain door (the back). They even were to have a separate little pool to swim in. Sounds all right, but would you let the New York Athletic Club build a building in the middle of Central Park? How about if they'd let you use it once in a while?

The important point was that the community was not consulted, as they had not been consulted with regard to the purchase of one hundred and fifty buildings and the eviction of ten thousand people over the past seven years. The gym served as a symbol for all Columbia expansion.

ARMBAND KEY

Green = for amnesty for protesting students.
Red = militant protesting students.

Baby Blue = against protest, but ostensibly for avoidance of violence.

White = faculty "keeping peace."

Black = mourning the passing of a cop-free, violence-free campus.

The Shit
Hits the Fan

Columbia used to be called King's College. They changed the name in 1784 because they wanted to be patriotic and *Columbia* means *America*. This week we've been finding out what America means.

Every morning now when I wake up I have to run through the whole thing in my mind. I have to do that because I wake up in a familiar place that isn't what it was. I wake up and I see blue coats and brass buttons all over the campus. ("Brass buttons, blue coat, can't catch a nanny goat" goes the Harlem nursery rhyme.) I start to go off the campus but then remember to turn and walk two blocks uptown to get to the only open gate. There I squeeze through the three-foot "out" opening in the police barricade, and I feel for my wallet to be sure I've got the two I.D.'s necessary to get back into my college. I stare at the cops. They stare back and see a red armband and long hair and they perhaps tap their night sticks on the barricade. They're looking at a radical leftist.

I wasn't always a radical leftist. Although not altogether

straight, I'm not a hair person either, and ten days ago I was writing letters to Kokomo, Indiana, for Senator McCarthy; my principal association with the left was that I rowed port on crew. But then I got involved in this movement and one thing led to another. I am not a leader, you understand. But leaders cannot seize and occupy buildings. It takes great numbers of people to do that. I am one of those great numbers. What follows is the chronicle of a single revolutionary digit.

Monday, April 22: A mimeograph has appeared around the campus charging SDS with using coercion to gain its political ends. SDS is for free speech for itself only, it is charged. SDS physically threatens the administration. SDS breaks rules with impunity while we (undefined) are subject to dismissal for tossing a paper airplane out a dorm window. Aren't you TIRED, TIRED, TIRED of this? Will Mark Rudd be our next dean? Do something about it. Come to the SDS rally tomorrow and *be prepared.* At first anonymous, the leaflet reappears in a second edition signed Students for a Free Campus. The jocks have done it again. As with the demonstrations against Marine campus recruiting in the spring of '67, threats of violence from the right will bring hundreds of the usually moderate to the SDS ranks just to align themselves against jock violence. I personally plan to be there, but I'm not up tight about it. At the boat house, a guy says he's for the jock position. Don't get me wrong, I say, I'm not against beating up on a few pukes, I just don't think you should stoop to their level by mimeographing stuff. We both go out and kill ourselves trying to row a boat faster than eight students from MIT will be able to.

Tuesday, April 23: Noon. At the sundial are 500 people ready to follow Mark Rudd (whom they don't particularly like because he always refers to President Kirk as "that shithead") into the Low Library administration building to demand severance from IDA, an end to gym construction, and to defy Kirk's recent edict prohibiting indoor demonstrations. There are around 100 counter-demonstrators. They are what Trustee Arthur Ochs Sulz-berger's newspaper refers to as "burly white youths" or "students of considerable athletic attainment"—jocks. Various deans and other father surrogates separate the two factions. Low Library is locked. For lack of a better place to go we head for the site of the gym in Morningside Park, chanting "Gym Crow must go." I do not chant because I don't like chanting.

I have been noncommittal to vaguely against the gym, but now I see the site for the first time. There is excavation cutting across the whole park. It's really ugly. And there's a chain link fence all around the hole. I don't like fences anyway so I am one of the first to jump on it and tear it down. Enter the New York Police Department. One of them grabs the fence gate and tries to shut it. Some demonstrators grab him. I yell "Let that cop go," partly because I feel sorry for the cop and partly because I know that the night sticks will start to flagellate on our heads, which they proceed to do. One of my friends goes down and I pull him out. He's on adrenaline now and tries to get back at the cops but I hold him, because I hit a cop at Whitehall and I wished I hadn't very shortly thereafter.* After the usual hassle, order is restored and the cops let Rudd mount a dirt pile to address us. As soon as he starts to talk he is drowned out by jackhammers but, at the request of the police, they are turned off. Rudd suggests we go back to the sundial and join with 300 demonstrators there, but we know that he couldn't possibly know whether there are 300 demonstrators there and we don't want to leave. He persists and we defer.

Back at the sundial there is a large crowd. It's clear we've got

---

* *In October of 1967, there was a series of "Stop the Draft Week" demonstrations at Whitehall, the Army Induction Center for Manhattan. At about 6 A.M. on a Thursday morning a blue cossack rode his lumbering steed at me on the sidewalk. It was just too early in the morning to get run over by a horse. I slugged him (the cop) in the thigh, which was as high as I could reach, and was immediately brought to bay and apprehended by a detective, who smashed me in the knee with a movie camera, and later let me go when he deduced from my name that I was Irish, which I'm not.*

something going. An offer comes from Vice-President Truman to talk with us in McMillin Theatre but Rudd, after some indecision, refuses. It seems we have the initiative and Truman just wants to get us in some room and bullshit till we all go back to sleep. Someone suggests we go sit down for awhile in Hamilton, the main college classroom building, and we go there. Sitting down turns to sitting-in, although we do not block classes. Rudd asks, "Is this a demonstration?" "Yes!" we answer, all together. "Is it indoors?" "Yes!"

An immediate demand is the release of the one student arrested at the park, Mike Smith, who might as well be named John Everyman, because nobody knows him. To reciprocate for Mike's detention, Dean Coleman is detained.

At four o'clock, like Pavlov's dog, I go to crew, assuring a longhair at the door that I'll be back. At practice it is pointed out to me that the crew does not have as many WASPS as it should have according to the population percentage of WASPS in the nation, so don't I think that crew should be shut down? I answer no, I don't think crew should be shut down.

Back at school at eight I prepared to spend the night at Hamilton. My friend Rock is there. We decide that we are absolutely bound to meet some girls or at least boys since there are 300 of them in the lobby. Every ten minutes he yells to me, "Hey, did you make any friends yet?" I say no each time, and he says that he hasn't either, but he's bound to soon.

I go upstairs to reconnoiter and there is none other than Peter Behr of Linda LeClair fame* chalking on the wall, " 'Up against the wall, motherfucker, . . .' from a poem by LeRoi Jones." I get some chalk and write "I am sorry about defacing the walls, but babies are being burned and men are dying, and this University is at fault quite directly." Also I draw some SANE symbols and then at 2:30 A.M. go to sleep.

---

* *See postscript on "Sex," page 146.*

Wednesday, April 24, 5:30 A.M. Someone just won't stop yelling that we've got to get up, that we're leaving, that the blacks occupying Hamilton with us have asked us to leave. I get up and leave. The column of evicted whites shuffles over to Low Library. A guy in front rams a wooden sign through the security office side doors and about 200 of us rush in. Another 150 hang around outside because the breaking glass was such a bad sound. They become the first "sundial people." Inside we rush up to Kirk's office and someone breaks the lock. I am not at all enthusiastic about this and suggest that perhaps we ought to break up all the Ming Dynasty art that's on display while we're at it. A kid turns on me and says in a really ugly way that the exit is right over there. I reply that I am staying, but that I am not a sheep and he is.

Rudd calls us all together. He looks very strained. He elicits promises from the *Spectator* reporters in the crowd not to report what he is about to say. Then he says that the blacks told us to leave Hamilton because they do not feel that we are willing to make the sacrifices they are willing to make. He says that they have carbines and grenades and that they're not leaving. I think that's really quite amazing.

We all go into Kirk's office and divide into three groups, one in each room. We expect the cops to come any moment. After an hour's discussion my room votes 29–16 to refuse to leave, to make the cops carry us out. The losing alternative is to escape through the windows and then go organize a strike. The feeling is that if we get busted, *then* there will be something to organize a strike about. The man chairing the discussion is standing on a small wooden table and I am very concerned lest he break it. We collect water in wastebaskets in case of tear gas. Some of it gets spilled and I spend my time trying to wipe it up. I don't want to leave somebody else's office all messy.

We check to see what other rooms have decided. One room is embroiled in a political discussion, and in the other everyone is busy playing with the office machines.

At about 8:30 A.M. we hear that the cops are coming. One hundred seventy-three people jump out the window. (I don't jump because I've been reading *Lord Jim.*) That leaves twenty-seven of us sitting on the floor, waiting to be arrested. In stroll an inspector and two cops. We link arms and grit our teeth. After about five minutes of gritting our teeth it dawns on us that the cops aren't doing anything. We relax a little and they tell us they have neither the desire nor the orders to arrest us. In answer to a question they say they haven't got MACE, either.

In through the window like Batman climbs Professor Orest Ranum, liberal, his academic robes billowing in the wind. We laugh at his appearance. He tells us that our action will precipitate a massive right-wing reaction in the faculty. He confides that the faculty had been nudging Kirk toward resignation, but now we've blown everything; the faculty will flock to support the President. We'll all be arrested, he says, and we'll all be expelled. He urges us to leave. We say no. One of us points out that Sorel said only violent action changes things. Ranum says that Sorel is dead. He gets on the phone to Truman and offers us trial by a tripartite committee if we'll leave. We discuss it and vote no. Enter Mark Rudd, through the window. He says that twenty-seven people can't exert any pressure, and the best thing we could do would be to leave and join a big sit-in in front of Hamilton. We say no, we're not leaving until our demands on the gym, IDA, and amnesty for demonstrators are met. Rudd goes out and comes back and asks us to leave again, and we say no again. He leaves to get reinforcements. Ranum leaves. Someone comes in to take pictures. We all cover our faces with different photographs of Grayson Kirk.

It's raining out, and the people who are climbing back in are marked by their wetness. Offered a towel by one of the new people, a girl pointedly says "No, thank you, I haven't been out." Rationally, we twenty-seven are glad that there are now 150 people in the office, but emotionally we resent them. As people dry out, the old and new become less easily differentiable, and I am trying for a field promotion in the movement so that I will not fade into the masses who jumped and might jump again.

The phone continues to ring and we inform the callers that we are sorry, but Dr. Kirk will not be in today because Columbia is under new management. After noon, all the phones are cut off by the administration.

At 3:45 I smoke my first cigarette in four months and wonder if Lenin smoked. I don't go to crew. I grab a typewriter and, though preoccupied by its electricness, manage to write:

The time has come to pass the time.

I am not having good times here. I do not know many people who are here, and I have doubts about why they are here. Worse, I have doubts about why I am here. (Note the frequency of the word *here*. The place I am is the salient characteristic of my situation.) It's possible that I'm here to be cool or to meet people or to meet girls (as distinct from people) or to get out of crew or to be arrested. Of course the possibility exists that I am here to precipitate some change at the University. I am willing to accept the latter as true or, rather, I am willing, even anxious, not to think about it any more. If you think too much on the second tier (think about why you are thinking what you think) you can be paralyzed.

I really made the conflicting-imperative scene today. I have never let down the crew before, I think. Let down seven guys. I am one-eighth of the crew. I am one-fiftieth of this demonstration. And I am not even sure that this demonstration is right. But I multiplied these figures by an absolute importance constant. I hate to hamper the hobby of my friends (and maybe screw, *probably* screw, my own future in it), I am sorry about that, but death is being done by this University and I would rather fight it than row a boat.

But then I may, they say, be causing a right-wing reaction and hurting the cause. Certainly it isn't conscionable to hold Dean Coleman captive. But attention is being gotten. Steps will be taken in one direction or another. The polls will fluctuate and the market quiver. Our being here is the cause of an effect. We're trying to make it good; I don't know what else to say or do. That is, I have no further statement to make at this time, gentlemen.

The news comes in that Avery Hall, the architecture school, has been liberated. We mark it as such on Grayson's map. At about 8 P.M. we break back into Kirk's inner office, which had been relocked by security when we gathered into one room when the cops came in the morning. The $450,000 Rembrandt and the TV have gone with the cops.

We explore. The temptation to loot is tremendous, middle-class morality notwithstanding, but there is no looting. I am particularly attracted by a framed diploma from American Airlines declaring Grayson Kirk a V.I.P., but I restrict myself to a few Grayson Kirk introduction cards. Someone finds a book on masochism behind a book on government. Someone else finds what he claims is Grayson's draft card and preparations are made to mail it back to the Selective Service. On his desk is an American Airlines jigsaw puzzle which has apparently been much played with.

We have a meeting to discuss politics and defense, but I sit at the door as a guard. A campus guard appears and, before I can do anything, surprises me by saying, "As long as you think you're right, fuck 'em." He hopes something good for him might come out of the whole thing. He makes eighty-six dollars a week after twenty years at the job.

I go down to the basement of Low, where the New York City Police have set up shop. There are approximately forty of them; there is precisely one of me. I ask one for the score of the Red Sox game. He seems stunned that a hippie faggot could be interested in such things, but he looks it up for me. Rained out.

I use the pay-phone to call a girl at Sarah Lawrence. I tell her how isolated I feel and how lonely I am and hungry and tired and she says oh. I explain that I'll be busted any minute and she says she knows that.

I return upstairs. One of these people who knows how to do

things has reconnected a phone, but he needs someone to hold the two wires together while he talks. I do it. I'll do anything to feel like I'm doing something.

Thursday, April 25: I get up and shave with Grayson Kirk's razor, use his toothpaste, splash on his after-shave, grooving on it all. I need something morale-building like this, because my revolutionary fervor takes about half an hour longer than the rest of me to wake up.

Someone asks if anyone knows how to fix a Xerox 3000, and I say yes, lying through my teeth. Another man and I proceed to take it apart and put it back together. To test it I draw a pierced heart with "Mother" in the middle and feed it to the machine. The machine gives back three of the same. Much rejoicing. Now we can get to work on Kirk's files. My favorite documents are a gym letter which ends with the sentence "Bring on the bull-dozers!" and a note to a Columbia representative to the land negotiations telling him to be careful *not* to mention to Parks Commissioner Hoving that the date for digging has been moved up. ("We don't want him to know that we decided on this over a year ago," the note explains.)

Since a bust does not seem imminent, I climb out the window and go to crew at four. I talk to the coach and we agree that I will sleep in Low but will show up for the bus to Cambridge the next morning if I'm not in jail.

When I get back from crew I have to run a police cordon and leap for the second-story ledge. A cop, much to my surprise, bothers to grab me and tries to pull me down, but some people inside grab me and pull me up.

A meeting is going on discussing defense. J.J. wants to pile art treasures on the windows so the cops will have to break them to get in. I'm for that. But he also wants to take poles and push cops off the ledge. When this is criticized he tries to make it clear that it will be done in a nonviolent way. A friend whispers to me that J.J. is SDS's answer to the jock. A guy in a red crash helmet begins to say that maybe we won't fight because we're not as manly as the blacks, but it is well known that he is loony as hell and he is shouted down in a rare violation of the democratic process. After two hours' debate it is decided to man the barricades until they start to fall, then gather in groups with locked arms and resist passively. A motion to take off all our clothes when the police arrive is passed, with most girls abstaining.

I get back to the Xerox and copy seventy-three documents, including clippings from *The New York Times*. I hear over the radio that Charles 37X Kenyatta and the Mau Maus are on campus. This does not surprise me.

J.J. is recruiting volunteers to liberate another building. He has thirty, male and female, and at 2 A.M. he's ready to move. I go out on the ledge to check for cops. There are only three, so we climb down and sprint to Mathematics Hall. There we are joined by twenty radicals who could no longer stand the Establishment-liberal atmosphere of the previously liberated Fayerweather Hall. We get inside and immediately pile up about 2000 pounds of furniture at the front door. Only then do we discover two housekeepers still in the building. They are quite scared but only say "Why didn't you tell us you were coming?" and laugh. We help them out a window and along a ledge with the aid of the just-arrived-press movie lights.

We hold the standard two-hour meeting to decide how to deal with the cops, whom we understand to be on their way. The meeting is chaired by Tom Hayden, who is an Outside Agitator. Reverend Starr, the Protestant counselor, tells us the best positions for firehoses and so on. Dean Alexander B. Platt is allowed in through the window. He looks completely dead. We consider capturing him, but no one has the energy, so we let him go after thanking him for coming. Professor Allen Westin, liberal, comes and offers us a tripartite committee which he has no authority to constitute and which we don't want. He is thanked and escorted to the window.

At 6 A.M. I go to sleep.

· · ·

Friday, April 26: I wake up at 8:55 and run to the crew bus and leave for MIT. From Cambridge I call my home in Marlboro. My mother asks me, "Are you on the side of the law-breakers in this thing?" For ten minutes we exchange mother talk and revolutionary rhetoric. She points out that neither Gandhi nor Thoreau would have asked for amnesty. I admit I haven't read them. But Gandhi had no Gandhi to read and Thoreau hadn't read Thoreau. They had to reach their own conclusions and so will I.

Saturday, April 27: I row a boat race and split. That wraps up the crew season—for me. On the MTA to Logan Airport a middle-aged man starts winking and smiling and gesticulating at my right lapel. Looking down, I see that I am wearing a broken rifle pin, symbol of the War Resisters' League. I tell him that it so happens I am on my way back to Columbia right now to carry on a Revolution. He thinks that's fine.

I get back to Math around 4:30 and sit down on the public-relations ledge over Broadway. People from a peace demonstration downtown are depositing money and food in a bucket at the bottom of a rope. Each time we haul it up and re-lower it we include I.D.'s for people who want to get into the campus. A remarkable number of cars toot their support, and when a bus driver pulls over to wave us a victory sign, ten people nearly fall off the ledge.

In the evening I discover that the electricity to the kitchen is cut off. I run downstairs and almost call for "someone important" but somehow I am unwilling to accept that kind of status relation. I tell several of my peers and one of them finds the fuse box and sets things right.

I volunteer for shopping. We buy twenty dollars of food for eighteen dollars (the merchants earlier had contributed food outright) and on the way back meet a gentleman who seems to belong to Drunken Faculty to Forget the Whole Mess. Someone whom I think of as a friend threatens to punch me because I am carrying food.

As the evening wears on I feel less useful and more alienated, so I assign myself the task of keeping the mayonnaise covered. After covering it twelve times I give up and decide to write home. I wonder whether the Paris Commune was this boring.

In the letter I try to justify rebelling on my father's money. I point out that one of the dangers of going to college is that you learn things, and that my present actions are much influenced by my Contemporary Civilization (C1001y) readings. After sealing the letter I realize that my conception of the philosophy of law comes not so much from Rousseau as from Fess Parker as Davy Crockett. I remember his saying that you should decide what you think is right and then go ahead and do it. Walt Disney really bagged that one; the old fascist inadvertently created a whole generation of radicals.

I discover a phone which has not been cut off and call my brother. As I am talking someone puts a piece of paper beside me and writes "This . . . phone . . . is . . . tapped." I address myself briefly to the third party and go on talking. It feels good to talk to someone on the outside, although it is disappointing to find out that the outside world is going on as usual.

Sunday, April 28: Four hours of meetings about tactical matters, politics, and reports from Strike Central. I begin to long for a benevolent dictator. It is announced that we are spending as much money on cigarettes as food. I wonder, as I look about me, whether Lenin was as concerned with the breast size of his revolutionary cohorts as I am. It is now daylight-saving time; under all the clocks are signs saying "It's later than you think."

I spend the day sunning and reading *Lord Jim* on the ledge. At 3 P.M. four fire trucks scream up and men go running onto the campus with axes. Some people think this is the bust, but it seems like the wrong public agency to me. It turns out to be a false alarm.

The neighborhood little kids are anxious and able to squeeze through the fences. I talk to some of them and they are all con-

versant with the issues and on our side. I conduct an informal
class in peace graffiti and distribute chalk.

The older brothers of these same kids are in the middle of
Broadway throwing eggs at us. This action—one of them tells
me later—is completely apolitical.

We have red flags flying from the roof. I explain to a cop on
the sidewalk below that these stand for revolution, not for com-
munism. He says yes, he remembers reading something about
that. I hope he is not referring to the *Daily News*. The *News*
charges us with vandalism and alcoholism. (Actually we voted
to bar both grass and liquor, and there was only one dissident,
named Melvin.) One cartoon, titled "Dancing to the Red
Tune," shows a beatnik and some sort of cave girl dancing as a
band sings "Louse up the campuses, yeah, yeah, yeah."

In the evening I walk into a room where there is a poetry reading. I don't want to be rude so I stay. A med student who looks
like Dr. Kildare reads a poem entitled "Ode to Mickey Mantle's
Five-hundredth HR."

Mutiny on the Bounty (Gable) is on TV and I find it in-
spirational, or at least amusing.

The student radio station, WKCR, announces that a clergyman is wanted in Fayerweather; a couple wants to get married.
This does not surprise me. Reverend Starr performs the ceremony
and says, "I pronounce you children of the new age." Shortly
after we hear it, we see a candlelight procession approaching.
The bride is carrying roses. She hands them to me and I pass
them inside. The demonstration peaks for me as I touch the
roses—I am stoned on revolutionary zeal. The newlyweds call
themselves Mr. and Mrs. Fayerweather.

I volunteer for jock-watch from 2:00 to 3:00 but do not wake
up the next man and stay out on the entrance window ledge until
five. I am to let no one in as we now have a population of 150
and we want a stable commune—no tourists. We even consider
a Stalinist purge to reduce the mouths to feed. Only tonight does
my roommate decide to occupy a building. I have about seven

degrees of disdain and contempt for him, but he got in before my watch. I stamp "Rush" on the hand of anyone who leaves. This allows them to get back in.

During my watch five guys in black cowls come by dragging a coffin and murmuring in Latin.

Monday, April 29: The Majority Coalition (read: jocks) have cordoned off Low and are trying to starve the demonstrators out. We decide to break the blockade. We plan tactics on a blackboard and go, shaking hands with those staying behind as though we might not be back. There are thirty of us with three cartons of food. We march around Low, making our presence known. Spontaneously, and at the wrong tactical place, the blacks in front jump into the jock line. I go charging through the gap with my box of grapefruit and quickly become upon the ground or, more accurately, on top of two layers of people and beneath two. I manage to throw three grapefruit, two of which make it. Then I become back where I started. Some blood is visible on both sides. Back at Math, some of our people say that the jocks they were fighting had handcuffs on their belts. Band-Aided noses abound and are a mark of distinction. We discuss alternative plans for feeding Low and someone suggests blockading the jocks—"If they run out of beer they're through." In the meantime, we can see hundreds of green armbands (for amnesty) throwing food up to the Low windows. We decide on a rope-and-pulley system between a tree and the Low windows, but there is some question about how to get the line up to the people in Low without the jocks grabbing it. When one kid suggests tying an end to a broom handle and throwing it like a harpoon, John (Outside Agitator) suggests we train a bird. A helicopter has already been looked into by Strike Central, but the FAA won't allow it. Finally we agree on shooting in a leader line with a bow and arrow.

A girl and myself are dispatched to get a bow. We go to the roof of the Barnard Library where the phys. ed. archery range is. We are in the midst of discovering how incredibly locked the cabinet is when a guard comes out on the roof. We crouch. He walks right past us. It would be just like TV were I not so preoccupied with it being just like TV. After ten minutes he finds us. The girl laughs coyly and alleges that oh, we just came up to spend the night. I am rather taken with the idea, but the guard is unmoved and demands our I.D.'s. This is our first bust.

Our second bust, the real one, begins to take shape at 2:30 A.M. We hear over WBAI that there are busloads of TPF (Tactical Police Force, Gestapo) at 156th and at 125th and that patrol cars are arriving from all precincts with four helmeted cops per auto. I am unimpressed. So many times now we've been going to be busted. It just doesn't touch me anymore. I assume that the cops are there to keep the Mau Maus out.

A girl comes up to me with some paper towels. Take these, she says, so you can wipe the vaseline (slows tear-gas penetration) off your face when you're in jail. I haven't got vaseline on my face. I am thinking that vaseline is a big petroleum interest, probably makes napalm, and anyway it's too greasy. I hear over the walky-talky that Hamilton has been busted and that the sundial people are moving to Low and Fayerweather to obstruct the police. I put vaseline on my face. I also put vaseline on my hands and arms and legs above the socks and a cigarette filter in each nostril and carefully refold my plastic-bag gas mask so I'll be able to put it on quickly with the holes at the back of my head so my hair will absorb the gas and I'll be able to breathe long enough to cool the cannister with a CO_2 fire extinguisher and pick it up with my asbestos gloves and throw it back at the cops. Someone tells me that he can't get busted or he'll miss his shrink again.

I take my place with seven others at the front barricade. All along the stairs our people are lined up, ready to hole up in the many lockable-from-within rooms on the three floors above me. We sing "We Shall Not Be Moved" and realize that something is ending. The cops arrive. The officer bullhorns us: "On behalf of the Trustees of Columbia University and with the authority vested in me . . ." That's as far as he is able to get, as we answer his question and all others with our commune motto—"Up against the wall, motherfuckers." We can't hold the barricade because the doors open out and the cops simply pull the stuff out. They have to cut through ropes and hoses and it takes them fifteen minutes before they can come through. All the while they're not more than thirty feet from me, but all I can do is watch their green-helmeted heads working. I shine a light in their eyes but Tom tells me not to and he's head of the defense committee so I stop.

At 4:00 A.M. the cops come in. The eight of us sit down on the stairs (which we've made slippery with green soap and water) and lock arms. The big cop says "Don't make it hard for us or you're gonna get hurt." We do not move. We want to make it clear that the police have to step over more than chairs to get our people out. They pull us apart and carry us out, stacking us like cord wood under a tree. The press is here so we are not beaten. As I sit under the tree I can see kids looking down at us from every window in the building. We exchange the "V" sign. The police will have to ax every door to get them out of those offices. They do. Tom Hayden is out now. He yells "Keep the radio on! Peking will instruct you!" When they have sixty of us out they take us to the paddy wagons at mid-campus. I want to make them carry us, but the consensus is that it's a long, dark walk and we'll be killed if we don't cooperate, so I walk. At the paddy wagons there are at least a thousand people cheering us and chanting "Strike! Strike! Strike!" We are loaded in a wagon and the doors shut. John tells a story about how a cop grabbed the cop that grabbed him and then said "Excuse me." We all laugh raucously to show an indomitable spirit and freak out the cops outside.

We are taken to the 24th precinct to be booked. "Up against the wall," we are told. I can't get over how they really do use the term. We turn and lean on the wall with our hands high, because that's what we've seen in the movies. We are told to can that shit and sit down. Booking takes two hours. Lieutenant Dave Bender is the plainclothesman in charge. He seems sternly unhappy that college turns out people like us. He asks John if he thinks he could be a policeman and John says no; he doesn't think he's cut out for it.

We are allowed three calls each. A fat officer makes them for us and he is a really funny and good man. He is only mildly displeased when he is duped into calling Dial-a-Demonstration. He expresses interest in meeting a girl named Janice when three of us give him her number, one as his sister, one as his girl friend, and one as his ex-wife.

We go downstairs to await transportation to court. A TPF man comes in escorting Angus Davis, who was on the sixth floor of Math and refused to walk down. He has been dragged down four flights of marble stairs and kicked and clubbed all the way. A two-inch square patch of his hair has been pulled out. Ben, Outside Agitator, yells, "You're pretty brave when you've got that club." The officer comes over and dares him to say that again. He says it again. The cop kicks for Ben's groin, but Ben knows karate and blocks it. John says to the cop, "Thank you, you have just proved Ben's point." This is sufficiently subtle not to further arouse the cop, and he leaves. A caged bus takes us all the way downtown to the tombs (the courthouse). The kid beside me keeps asking me what bridge is this and what building is that. Finally he recognizes something and declares that we are going to pass his grandmother's house. I am busy trying to work a cigarette butt through the window grate so that I can litter from a police bus. Arriving, we drive right into the building; a garage door clamps down behind us.

Our combs and keys are confiscated so that we won't be able to commit suicide. In the elevator to the cells a white cop tells us we look like a fine bunch of men—we ought to be put on the front lines in Vietnam. Someone says that Vietnam is here, now. As we get out I look at the black cop running the elevator for some sort of reaction. He says "Keep the faith."

He said "Keep the faith," I say, and everyone is pleased. We walk by five empty cells and then are jammed into one, thirty-four of us in a 12x15 room. We haven't slept in twenty-four hours and there isn't even space for all of us to sit down at one time.

Some of our cellmates are from Avery. They tell us how they were handcuffed and dragged downstairs on their stomachs. Their shirts are bloody.

After a couple of hours we start to perk up. We bang and shout until a guard comes, and then tell him that the door seems to be stuck. Someone screams "All right, all right, I'll talk." It is pointed out that you don't need tickets to get to policemen's balls. We sing folk songs and "The Star-Spangled Banner." They allowed one of us to bring in a recorder and he plays Israeli folk music.

A court officer comes and calls a name. "He left," we say. Finally he finds the right list.

We are arraigned before a judge. The Outsiders are afraid they will be held for bail, but they are released on their own recognizance, like the rest of us, except they have some form of loitering charge tacked on to the standard second-degree criminal trespassing.

Back at school I eat in a restaurant full of police. As audibly as possible I compose a poem entitled "Ode to the TPF." It extolls the beauty of rich wood billies, the sheen of handcuffs, the feel of a boot on your face.

Meeting a cellmate, I extend my hand to him and he slaps it. I have to remember that—handslaps, not shakes, in the Revolution.

Tom Hayden is in Chicago now. As an Outside Agitator, he has a lot of outsides to agitate in. Like the Lone Ranger, he didn't even wave good-bye, but quietly slipped away, taking his silver protest buttons to another beleaguered campus.

Everyone is organizing now—moderates, independent radicals, Liberated Artists, librarians. And the Yippies are trying to sue the University for evicting us from our homes which we owned by virtue of squatters' rights. You can hardly move for the leaflets here. Except at Barnard. The Barnard girls are typing their papers and getting ready to go to Yale for the weekend.

We are on strike, of course. There are "liberation classes" but the scene is essentially no more pencils, no more books.

I saw a cellist math major in Chock Full O' Nuts looking alone. Liberation classes won't help him. He is screwed. Every Revolution leaves a trail of screwed drifting in its wake.

The campus is still locked, although I think you could get in with a Raleigh coupon as an I.D. today. That's our latest issue; a liberated campus should be open. We want free access by June so we can open the summer school under our own aegis.

A particularly thick swatch of air pollution drifted by today and a lot of people thought the gym site was burning. That did not surprise me. Nothing surprises me any more.

Aftermath

Saturday, May 4: A sundial rally drags on and on. Finally it is brought to our attention that the corporate power elite are chortling with joy over the split between the black and white radical movements in this country. That they would hate to see us get together. That we therefore must get together. We are going to Harlem. The speaker says he knows that as white men we are probably afraid to go down the hill to the other world, but we should do it. He chants "To Harlem, to Harlem," and goes there, followed by at least five hundred people yelling the same thing.

I am carrying a sign reading "Columbia: Get Out of Harlem." I consider this somewhat paradoxical, because after all I am a Columbian and I am walking *into* Harlem. A black woman on the sidewalk says "What the hell do you mean, 'Get out of Harlem'?" My heart sinks. We look like an invading army and no one wants us here and what are we doing here, anyway?

But when we arrive at 125th and 7th Avenue we are greeted by a troop performing African dances to throbbing drums and everything is cool and groovy and I'm really glad to be there. The leader of the dancers teaches us to say "Hello, how are you" in Nigerian. When it begins to rain, the dancers begin an anti-rain dance and it stops. The leader concludes with a plug for his studio, which teaches dance, song, drums, and karate.

We are addressed by a number of community organizers. One of them puts down whites and adds, "I know that doesn't sound right. I don't care. I'm mad. I'm mad because I'm poor." He says a lot of things that make me uncomfortable, but I figure perhaps I ought to feel uncomfortable and anyway he ends up by exchanging "V's" with us. The message of the rally is that the blacks don't want direct white help because the whites come in from Westchester and talk about rats and roaches, and then go back to Westchester and leave the blacks with the rats and roaches. We should go back and do our thing, and the blacks will do theirs, and together, in a parallel way, we'll bring down the Establishment.

After the rally, we all, black and white, march back to Columbia chanting "Beep Beep! Bang Bang! Ungowah! Black Power!" and have another rally, but the gates are locked, most of the New York City Police Force is there, and it's raining, so we break up. Someone yells at a man in a patrol car, "The only thing worse than a cop is an Uncle Tom plainclothesman."

Saturday, May 11: I get a haircut and make a command appearance at home. I am told by my father that, as an ex-con, I will be a hard-core unemployable for the rest of my life. Promising not to get in any more trouble, I return to Columbia University in the City of New York.

Friday, May 17: There is a "mammoth rally" in the afternoon at Low. It isn't really *that* mammoth, but the crowd is swelled by a fair number of high-school girls making the scene. Rap Brown's attorney speaks and makes a memorable reference to David Susskind as "that ivy-covered salami." Of course, everyone else and all his friends speak too, but nobody leaves because we've been promised a big surprise announcement at the end. We get it. It seems that a community group has seized and barricaded a building that Columbia has been forcing people out of. They won't leave until Columbia promises to restore the building to the community. We are going there. We march down Broadway, explaining in unison that "the streets belong to the People." Exactly where we are going has not been announced, so that the police won't get there before we do. It turns out to be 618 West 114th Street. We mill around outside to show our support and make a bust logistically more difficult. A few jocks arrive, but they are obviously just trying to keep up appearances. Twice I hold back a jock who is starting a fight, and twice he lets me hold him. Clearly, the old socko is gone.

In the evening, a few police arrive to seal off the street. But I'm confident that there will be no bust until the usual time, about 3 A. M., so when it gets to be late and cold I go home and go to bed.

At about 3 A. M. Rock wakes me up for the bust. The TPF are rolling in. I don't want to be arrested again so I decide I'll take this one in from the roof of my dormitory, which faces 114th. The roof is crowded with kids, some with binoculars. One is yelling "Scorecard! Scorecard! Can't tell the cops from the pukes without a scorecard." Hundreds of helmeted cops are lined up along Broadway, which leads me to reminiscences about police brutality. Suddenly a boy beside me turns and, looking me straight in the eye, says, "There is no police brutality." There is a hush. Everyone falls silent. "What do you mean?" I ask. He answers only that we guys are all stupid and he's sick of it. We all begin talking again, and no one throws him off the roof.

The police march on 618. We try hard not to yell down at them, because if their poor, human, volatile tempers flare up, it will be the sitters-in who will suffer. We count twelve paddy wagons lined up, as if at the drive-in teller window of a bank, each making its withdrawal. The newsreel floodlights are on, and we can see all the little figures holding up their little hands in the

"V" sign. It's quite an effect. It's all over in an hour and, while everyone is glad there was no violence, the prevalent opinion is that this was the dullest bust we've ever been to.

Saturday, May 18: I go to a farewell crew banquet and drink beer with all the guys. *Drink beer.* Just like in the good old college days.

Tuesday, May 21: As a result of the proliferation of my diary in *New York* magazine, I am now a qualified spokesman for the Columbia strikers, the international peace movement, and everyone in the world younger than thirty. Nonetheless, I agree to go on a Mutual Radio Network interview with some misgivings concerning my expertise on its subject, "The Generation Gap." It turns out, however, that the interviewer lives but three doors from Mark Rudd back in New Jersey, and this, coupled with my absolute inability to conceive of anyone listening to such a program, allays my nervousness to the point where I can go ahead and incriminate myself on seven counts of everything. When it's all over I am too embarrassed to ask about money and therefore get none, not even cab fare. This is The Big City.

I take the subway back and arrive at campus at about 5 P.M., just in time for the meeting with our lawyers. But there is no one there. Enquiring as to what is going on here, I find that everybody is over at Hamilton where a sit-in is now in progress. The facts, as they are related to me, are that Dean Platt has sent letters to Rudd and others demanding their appearance before him; that they have exercised their right (Constitutional) not to appear while their case is in court; that they have consequently been suspended; and that everyone else in the world has shown up to protest. That's good enough for me. We're nearing the bottom of the barrel in unarrested radical manpower, so there are only about 150 sitting-in in the building, but I join the let's say 1500 standing outside in non-trespassing support. Every so often I get hit with eggs, which a small group of jocks are having good clean fun throwing. Since they have no arguments and no support for their arguments (of which they have none), they have no recourse but to assault us like this and sing fight songs—that's right, fight songs. They are standing there—I beg you to believe this—throwing eggs and singing "Roar, Lion, Roar" all the while. They sing "Who Owns New York?" (C-O-L-U-M-B-I-A) which I think is particularly amusing, because it is precisely our point that Columbia is such a huge real-estate enterprise (owning four percent of New York, to be exact). They top it all off by launching into "America." We join them in this one.

I leave Hamilton to aid in the construction of barricades at either end of College Walk. This is one of the more purely symbolic acts I have ever indulged in, since there are at least seven other gates and countless tunnels through which the cops can get in. At the Amsterdam Avenue end we are having trouble barricading one of the gates. The cops, who are awaiting orders just outside, offer us all sorts of advice, interspersed with statements impugning the value of a college education if we can't figure out how to wedge a gate shut. Finally one of them digs into his pocket and offers me a padlock, which I accept with some thanks and considerable amazement. Unfortunately, it doesn't fit, so I give it back.

At 2:30 A.M. the cops are inside Hamilton, having emerged from the tunnels within. The arrestees are removed through the tunnels, but there is a large confrontation between demonstrators and police at the doors. The police are keeping the demonstrators from getting into the building but the demonstrators, on the other hand, are keeping the police from getting out on the campus.

Near Schermerhorn Hall, a crowd gathers to attempt to hold up the paddy wagons. People are incredibly mad. These navy-blue masses may be the Law, but to us they are the same bunch of animals who, totally unprovoked, beat up 150 people at the first bust, and they're back, they're back on our campus, and we want to get them the hell out. I see bricks, signs, and a potted tree hurled onto police cars parked seventy feet below us. The cars are empty. I don't think anyone wants to hurt policemen, but at least we can make their visit cost them something in technology.

Elsewhere a group of thirty cops has come through a gate which leads, via the hallways of two dormitories, onto campus. As they begin to emerge from the dorm a group of about two hundred students confronts them screaming "Cops must go!" and meaning it. I see one of my more moderate friends at the front of the group and just go up to him and shake his hand. Then we all start moving toward the cops. They back up a little and we move forward a little, and we move forward a lot and they back up a lot until we've marched them backwards right off the campus. We slam the gate between us.

The Fire Department makes the scene, since smoke seems to be pouring out of one of the classroom buildings, and I sit around and watch them for a while. So do a lot of other kids. Those extension ladders are amazing. Someone yells "Hooray for the Fire Department! *They* don't beat people up."

There is a big crowd at the sundial, so I go there to see what's up. Dean Platt is up. He has a bullhorn, and says it's his sad duty to announce that the campus will be cleared by the police. Everyone is to leave or return to his dormitory. Some kid rushes up and grabs the bullhorn from him. A strike leader apologizes profusely for this, which I think is sort of funny, in a way.

One minute, at the most, after his announcement, there are shouts that the TPF are coming through the barricade. I figure that I didn't *really* have time to leave the campus, did I; in fact, I might not even have heard the announcement. I rush to the falling barricade at Amsterdam Avenue.

A huge column of TPF are trudging in. Their front ranks are already right on top of us. I keep yelling walk, don't run, to everybody. We can back up slowly; we mustn't panic and trample each other. Suddenly the TPF are unleashed. They charge us, swinging their clubs. I have to turn and run and after about six steps I trip over someone who has tripped over someone else. I curl up into a rolling ball and watch a lot of blue legs run past me. When I get up, I'm right in the middle of the police. Two of them single me out and start chasing me with clubs raised. I run like a thief for the other side of the campus, for Broadway, for *away*, that's all, far away. A cop in front of me turns and waits for me. I notice that he has his weight on the balls of his feet, his club parallel to the ground, ready for me to go either way. I'm thinking what a goddamn shame it is that I'm wearing my goddamn loafers because I can't run very well in them. I veer off to the right and he gets a good backhand stroke into my left calf, but I don't fall down. I see a first-aid circle and jump into it like goals in tag. Twenty feet away a kid has tripped and two cops are on him, one kicking, one clubbing. I run down to help him (which consists of yelling "Hey, leave him alone"), but the cops are through with him. A stretcher is brought but he says "That's all right, I'm fine." There is blood streaming down his face. I think that he obviously doesn't know what he is talking about. He is put on the stretcher. Someone, I think he's the head of the Columbia cheerleaders, is standing nearby saying "Oh my God, Oh my God," not addressing God really, but just sort of saying it over and over. I resolve that nothing is going to get me off this campus tonight.

The cops are regrouping, so I have a chance to join a concentration of students on South Field. They rush us again, but I manage to get into the lobby of Ferris Booth Hall. The TPF are right on the patio, separated from us only by glass doors. We see them putting tape over their badge numbers.

We withdraw to the auditorium to hold a meeting about whether to leave, or stay on campus and get arrested and suspended. Nothing is decided. It's up to the individual. When we come out, the cops have withdrawn to the center of the campus, so I go outside. It is getting light.

I'm standing with some friends when I notice two husky grey-suited gentlemen walking up to a long-haired kid standing alone

on the edge of the lawn with a camera. Suddenly they run up
to him and knock him to the ground and start punching him and
dragging him away. He screams "Leave me alone, please, I was
just standing there!" They're plainclothesmen. I yell "Come on,
there's just two of them. Let's get him back." Five of us start to
run towards them. I am terribly frightened and I don't know
what I'm going to do when I get there. Someone behind us
throws an empty Seven-up can which bounces off one of the
plainclothesmen's heads. Right off his grey crew cut. He yells
"Get back or somebody's going to get killed," and reaches to his
side, pulls out a gun and waves it at us. I yell "He's got a gun"
and bolt away, not knowing whether or not I am going to hear
a bang.

I stop alongside a friend who was in on this episode. We light
cigarettes. I'm thinking it's lucky my cigarettes are Marlboros,
with the crush-proof box, or they would have been ruined by
now. He tells me that our mutual acquaintance Larry was
clubbed inside his dorm, on the mezzanine floor, as he stood with
his key in his door. We laugh about what an amazing loser Larry
is, how that was bound to happen to him. I'm thinking it's great
that we're able to stand and joke with each other right after we
almost got killed.

A bunch of plainclothesmen rush our group and we run into
Carmen Hall. As soon as they leave, we come out again, and they
rush us again, and we come out again. It reminds me of a game
of red-light.

One time we pile up at the door and one of us doesn't quite
make it in. Three cops grab him in the doorway and try to drag
him away, but we grab him too and try to pull him in. It's a
stalemate; he's bent over, not going either way. One of the cops
takes the opportunity to punch him again and again in the back
of the head. I cup my hands over the back of his head. The
puncher grabs my arm and bends it around the door frame and
yells "Let's drag this guy out," which they start to do. I extend
my free arm in and say as clearly as I can, "Take my hand, they're

dragging me out." Someone does and everyone gets in. The kid who was pounded is standing there saying "Whew," that's all. I can't figure out how he can continue to exist, how he can breath in and breath out and beat his heart and just continue as a person. I don't see how anyone can be in such danger without ending his self. For my part, I put my face in my hands and think, "I am putting my face in my hands."

At 8 A.M. I go to bed.

At 11 A.M. the phone rings. Would I like to be on the "New York" show? They can put me behind a screen so I won't have to blow my pseudonym. I say sure, I'll go on, but never mind about the screen.

I arrive at the studio building and walk right in, past a long line of high-school girls waiting to see a show. I have a copy of *New York* magazine with me and open it conspicuously to my diary. I am sent to make-up, where I meet the star of the show, Bill Leighton, whom I recognize as the typical Joe Moderator of countless afternoon programs.

The show begins, and as I wait at the side of the stage I notice that the audience is composed of the girls I passed outside. One of them seems to be mooning over me, just because I'm going to be on the tube. Where was she before I became famous, that's what I want to know.

After ten minutes of hair-styling tips, a few ads, and a song, I am introduced. Applause. The show is live; I'd be nervous if I were awake. Before we get into a discussion, some newsreel footage of the previous night's bust is shown. The greater part of it consists of two cops kindly ministering to an injured man. I point out that the injured one is a plainclothesman. Laughter. Bill Leighton asks me why I've decided to reveal my real name. I say it's because after what I saw last night, I don't care what Columbia does to me, which is not entirely true. Some discussion ensues, during which the female guest star reveals herself to be almost as opinionated as she is uninformed. She calls me an overindulged child. She turns out to be David Susskind's wife. Leon Bibb, the singer, sympathizes with me, as does, surprisingly, Mr. Leighton. Finally I am asked, "Well, Jim, where does it all go from here?" I allow as how I don't know—I'm not advocating this—but we might begin to emulate the French. Tsk, tsk, boo from the high schoolers, who have brought a cake for Mr. Leighton.

Back at campus, I pick up a release from the Columbia U. Office of Public Information. It's always interesting to see what nineteenth-century oligarchs would, and do, have to say about the situation. The leaflet lists every detail of campus damage, down to the exact number of bricks dug from the paths, but makes one salient and curious omission. It says, "Ferris Booth—glass front doors broken, cause uncertain," when any number of witnesses, including the victim herself, could testify that the police pushed a girl through the door. That's how the door was broken.

In the afternoon there is a rally of at least 1000 people. Mark Rudd tells how there were so many cops surrounding him that "They must have thought they had Jesse James." Another speaker stresses that "We are not out to destroy the University; we are out to recapture it."

An SDS'er relates another episode in the continuing story of Columbia's incredible real-estate deals. Consolidated Edison and Columbia, the story goes, were bidding for a piece of land. It was just a little friendly competition within the family, though, since President Kirk is on the board of directors of Con. Ed. Con. Ed. ended up with the land, but wasn't ready to build. So, rather than pay taxes on it for a year, they sold it to the non-profit institution Columbia for one dollar. Later, Columbia sold it back, for one dollar. An immense marble Edison building memorializes the transaction.

A Greek chorus of "Strike! Strike! Strike!" punctuates the speaking. I still don't like chanting.

Next, the Strike Committee asks for donations. So far they've used about three million sheets of paper and burned out six mimeograph machines.

Finally, a Mr. Higgerson of the Morningside Renewal Council

(anti-expansion), who is seventy-four years old and considered by everyone to be a real stone groove, belts out in his best FDR voice, "What institution has thrown out 8000 people in the last ten years? (Columbia.) What institution refuses to stop building the gym? (Same.) That is the institution that we are fighting today for the purpose—yes—of turning things upside down, which is another way of saying Revolution."

As we are dispersing from the rally a young man hands out some kind of circular. The fellow in front of me takes one, looks at it, says "Bullshit," and gives it back. It is an Office of Public Information release.

Wednesday evening I go out for a walk around the campus, to see if it's still all there. At Low Plaza there is a large group of people neatly arranged on the steps, chatting, looking for all the world like the Yale chorus between numbers. I ask an SDS man what's going on and he says people are arguing with cops. He says it's stupid, they're stupid, they beat our friends bloody. I figure I'll take a look anyway, to try to learn the plainclothesmen's faces.

"When a policeman gives you a massage," one of the cops is saying, "he does it like a pro, which he is, but a jock does it like an amateur and you get hurt. That's the fundamental reason Kirk called the cops, to keep you from getting hurt and to keep the jocks out of jail."

It occurs to me that this is just absurd enough so that it might very well have been Dr. Kirk's reasoning.

"The reason the police are such an issue," he continues, "is that you've got a lot of revolutionaries who think they're not supposed to get hurt in a revolution. I can hardly see Lenin complaining about police brutality."

Once again I wonder what old V.I. actually did have to say about these things. I'm told that this "plainclothesman" is a history professor from NYU. This makes me feel a little bit silly, and I go away and sit down.

A huge firecracker goes off. The boom drives away the talking and then the talking, tentatively at first, drifts back. Laughter escapes from the hum of conversation. People are enjoying the night. You can even see some stars.

Campus security guards wheel up two big tanks of coffee and a load of sandwiches to the steps of Low. No sooner do they recognize the difficulty they'll have with the stairs than two jocks appear and carry the stuff up for them, carry the food to the New York police in the basement of Low.

I'm making a note of this and they see that I am, and they say, "Look, it's one of those unbiased reporters from *Spectator*." I inform them that I am not with *Spectator*. "Then let's hear your unbiased report." I start to read, but they leave to go chat with the guards. They seem to be on a first-name basis with them.

I'm afraid, walking in dark places. I'm afraid I might get mugged by a cop.

Near Schermerhorn five jocks come up to me and tell me that the cops want me to leave. I tell them "This is really strange. I mean I could see you beating me up if you wanted to."

"Why would we do that? You guys are the ones who use violence," one of them says, moving very close and big to me.

As is my wont in these situations, I begin enumerating all the jocks who are some of my best friends, really. I say, "I haven't got anything against j——, I mean against you guys."

I single out the one who seems the most reasonable, that is, the one who has the least psychic need to pound me. I ask him what he considers his function to be. Some kind of amateur cop? He says "No, we're . . . we're . . ."

"Patrolling the campus on your own?" I volunteer.

"Yuh," he affirms, "patrolling the campus on our own."

"Oh *well*, I can see *that*," I say.

Another of the jocks suggests that they go get the two cops who are sitting several hundred feet away. I indicate that I'd be interested to see if they could get them; I'll wait.

They get them and the cops tell us all to leave. Another striker who has just joined me refuses to leave, says "Where to? How far? This is my campus." A cop shoves him with his night stick. I stare at his badge, scanning it repeatedly, trying to dis-

cern what numerals are represented on it, in case he starts clubbing the kid. "Two-six-six-six-eight," says the cop. "Now get out
of here."

Walking away, I ask one of the jocks if he's in engineering.
(Jocks are supposed to be in engineering.)

"Yuh," he says. "My teachers teach me to make napalm. I
love it. But I'd rather go to liberation classes and learn good
things like how to sap money from the economy."

It's around 1:30 but the sundial arguments continue. It takes
me fully five minutes to figure out who's on what side.

The man on the right says, "How can a small group of people
tell everybody what's right and what's wrong?"

The man on the left says, "Aren't the Trustees a small group
who do just that?"

The man on the right says, "I don't want IDA and I don't
want you. You're on a fellowship. You're accepting money from
that oppressive society."

The man on the left says, "If you don't like it here you can
leave, they say, but who makes this place?"

A lot of people support the one I interpret to be the leftist.
They finally give up and one says of the I-suppose-rightist, "He's
a typical American. He doesn't want to hear the truth." I've got
to hand it to the guy though. He was one against ten and he
didn't know a damn thing, but he took 'em all on.

On 114th Street I am disconcerted to find a bottle smashing
to the sidewalk beside me. Carmen Hall, the dorm, and Beta,
the fraternity, seem to have escalated their perpetual animosity
in accordance with the times. Kids are throwing bottles from
thirteen stories up onto the House's front steps, on which the
jocks are standing. The jocks charge into Carmen and tear apart
two rooms, chosen at random.

Thursday, May 23: I go to a rally. Reverend Starr says "There is
now in effect a local pacification program," which I think is a
very apt analogy, a truly fine analogy. No one can say the two-
hour rally was worthless.

Later, in a restaurant, I'm sitting at the counter reading a magazine after I've finished eating and the counterman tells me to leave. "I'm not trying to be offensive," he says, "but I don't like you guys." I wonder why. I try not to let it bother me. I don't leave a tip.

It is written in the Carmen elevator, "Buy eggs and throw them at the jocks at nine tonight."

In the evening I go to a meeting of all those who have received or expect to receive disciplinary letters. That qualifies about 900 students to attend, but there are only twenty-five there.

I notice that the cancer magnates are really cleaning up in these revolutionary days. There are hundreds of cigarettes on the floor.

A kid points out that we've come to the big crunch. If you don't go to the dean you're suspended and you have the draft and prison. We have to decide now whether we're in this as students or as people, whether we're willing to be professional revolutionaries for the rest of our lives. I figure one could do worse than being a pro revolutionary. It's a living.

Plans are made to get 500 people to refuse to see the dean and then 1000 to demand the same punishment as the 500. Either they back down or they suspend 1500 kids. "We win either way."

Back at my room I feel depressed but I can't go to bed because I only got up at 3 P.M. I'm going to be on the tube (Allen Burke called), but I'm depressed. That's funny. Maybe I should read Galbraith so I'll be prepared to field questions on the military-industrial complex.

I decide to write home. I don't recognize my parents as an ultimate authority, but I'm really for them all the way, and they're for me, in their own repressive, negative, parental way. Anyway, sometimes the thing that I do is write to them.

I write, "Although I was not really involved in the Tuesday night bust, I saw things, bloody horrible things, cruel unnecessary things that this University did to its students, and I've decided that they can do their worst to me and I won't mind." I don't mail the letter.

. . .

Friday, May 24: I go down to see Allen Burke's booking secretary. She is wearing a peace symbol, and she's pretty hippielooking, and she says she's on my side. She says Allen Burke is kind and liberal.

On the way home I come upon a police recruiting table in the subway. After steeling myself for the encounter, I walk up and ask the cop if they let leftists into the force. He says "Lefthanded, right-handed, we take them all." I try an opposite tack: "Are there many Birchers among the cops?" "No, the police have no political affiliation."

I pick up "This is Your Policeman" Public Information Bulletin No. 5. Under "His Code of Ethics" it says, "I will enforce the law . . . never employing unnecessary force or violence and never accepting gratuities." I guess the cops at the Tuesday bust must have had this in mind, because I didn't see any of them taking tips.

I talk to some more cops back at Columbia, but I'm so preoccupied with acting the regular guy, commenting on girls who walk by and Columbia basketball and everything, that I can't argue very well, not even when one cop says "My country right or wrong"—comes right out and says it.

I tell my roommate about Burke's secretary and he says that she probably has a drawer full of different political pins and a button she can push to turn the pictures on the wall to Johnson or Mao or Hitler, depending on who walks in.

I ask some Strike committeemen whether I should go on the show. They suggest that I tell Burke what he can do with himself. But I'm ambivalent; it's hard to turn down the national tube.

Monday, May 28: Everybody has told me bad things about the Burke show, so I telephone the secretary with my regrets. I won't go on. Pained, she says, "Look, Jim, you can't do this to me." She knows what I've heard, but that's all past—Burke's trying for a new, rational image. Anyway, she blew her whole weekend looking for someone for me to debate. It was so hard—everyone agreed with me. If I renege, she'd be left holding the bag. She didn't think *I'd* be afraid. Besides, they've got some great guests on the same show with me. They've got Rex Reed. "Okay, okay," I say, trying to make her feel better, "In that case I'll go on." I hang up. "Who's Rex Reed?" I ask my roommate, my friends, people on the street. No one knows.

Wednesday, May 29: I've studied everything. I'm prepared to put down the conservative student with unassailable facts like "The summary suspension of those arrested May 22 was a violation of: the procedures of the Joint Discipline Committee, the 1st, 5th and 14th amendments, Article I, sec. 6 of the New York State Constitution, ch. 8, par. 85, 1. 1810 of the Columbia University Charter, and the tradition of American jurisprudence separating judge and prosecutor." I've memorized quotes from the Constitution, David Truman and the Bible. I have a practice debate with the cab driver on the way to the studio.

Five minutes before going on Mr. Burke assures me that, since he knows nothing about Columbia, he will stay completely out of the discussion—just moderate.

For the first few seconds of the show I am too nervous to speak, but then I become involved and settle down. I can handle my opponent, I can handle the almost unanimously negative questions from the audience, I can try to handle the invective of Mr. Burke, who contrary to assurances soon becomes my antagonist. But I have some problem with the station breaks, which always follow Burke's most cutting remarks, and with an overly enthusiastic member of the audience who jumps up to lead applause after each remark against me, effectively preventing me from answering them. It turns out that this clapper is the prompter who cues the audience when to applaud, according to the instructions given them before the show.

I am dubbed a "deranged anarchist" and Mr. Burke concludes

the show with the suggestion that I stick to panty raids, which he says are "more constructive." I suppose he could have been worse.

Monday, June 3: This is my return date at court. I'm late, and I can't find the building. I ask a lot of people where it is, wondering whether they think I'm some kind of clerk, or whether they appreciate the fact that I'm a political criminal.

I finally get there in time to wait an hour for the judge, who turns out to be at least 105 years old. The bailiff impresses me with his verbal volume and fluency. He says "All rise," and then starts auctioning tobacco or something.

My lawyer eventually stands up, on behalf of the first group of students, and abjectly admits that he hasn't done his homework. He's just not prepared for a preliminary hearing yet. "The People is ready today," says the prosecutor, rather smugly, I think. The judge gives the defense two days to get ready.

There are about eighty of us being called to judgment. We are divided into small groups according to who our arresting officer was. A succession of Lawyers' Guild attorneys rise to present impassioned and more or less eloquent appeals for putting off the trial for at least sixty days. They want to raise certain Constitutional issues regarding dissent and the Bill of Rights, and they need time to get their stuff together. The judge is not impressed; in fact there is reason to believe that he may not be alive. In my group our lawyer asks that at least in the case of one student, who must return to Wisconsin to work on his family's farm, the trial be put off until September. "June 20," says the judge. "The People are entitled to a swift adjudication of this." Personally, I doubt that the people give a damn. However, Frank Hogan, the District Attorney, is probably very interested. He's a Trustee of Columbia.

Tuesday, June 4: Strike supporters congregate at five separate rallies and converge on 115th Street to hear speeches. The line of marchers stretches for blocks. It's so long that it can accommodate four or five different chants simultaneously, although "Pigs must go!," directed at the cops, doesn't catch on. At 3:30 someone holds a radio up to the mike. "The Times They are A-changin'!," a pacifist marching song by Dylan, is being played, and we are told that this is the signal for graduates (who brought transistors into the Cathedral) to walk out. I expect to see twenty or thirty people emerge, but at least 300 stream out. Oh man, what a day, what a fine day. I wonder if anyone is left inside.

We all go to a counter-commencement and hear a lot of bourgeois-revisionist drivel, with the exception of the Great Shrink Erich Fromm, who says that low-grade psychosis can *help* people function in certain societies, that a society in which human affairs can be discussed without corresponding human emotions is mad, that in a crazy society the sane are supposed to have lost their minds, that anyone who does not lose his mind over certain affairs never had a mind to lose.

A lot of other things happen, but I really don't want to talk about them, because I am actually writing this at 4 A.M. Wednesday, June 5, and I just heard over the radio that Kennedy has been shot. Again. This is really no novelty, you know, because people get shot every day, and bombed and burned and blown up. But no one cares about that. I mean they don't really mind, because it's a question of flags and things and anyway, people aren't really shot; fire is directed at their positions. And they're not really people; they're troops. There aren't even dead men; only body counts. And the degree of deadness isn't always too bad; sometimes it's light or moderate instead of heavy. We'll stick it out, don't worry. We'll stick it out because it's a question of honor and thank God we only hear about it once a day, and then it's quickly followed by some broad telling you how groovy some gasoline is and how you can get laid practically as much as you want if you use it. President Johnson's a fool anyway. The old fool's up against the wall. He's practically crazy. Everyone knows that. Even crazy people. Everyone.

Summer in the City and Other Downs

Wednesday, June 19: I went to Washington, D.C., for the rich people's march in support of the Poor People's Campaign. You are supposed to come away from these affairs with a renewed commitment and sense of purpose. I came away with two girls' addresses and a slight tan.

Thursday, June 20: Went to court a second time to be told I must go a third time in September. That's good because when they start to nail us in the fall, the whole student body will be around to watch, and act.

Friday, June 21: I saw a good-looking, interesting, intelligent girl in the subway train and, of course, knew I would never see her again unless I said something. But I didn't really know what to say, and anyway I was dressed in a cruddy old sweatshirt. I mean, *wearing* a sweatshirt is fine, but I wasn't wearing it, I just happened to have it on. I could have cited the fantastic odds

against our ever having been in the same place at the same time.
We both got off at the same stop. Encouraged by fate in action,
I asked her for a cigarette and tried to get her to know me, but
she pointed out that she was waiting for someone and said
good-bye before I was leaving. I said, "I'm writing a book. Look
for yourself in it."

Monday, June 24: I wrote: "Morning—Cox Commission; Noon
—Liberation School opens" on my calendar, but that is the
extent of my acquaintance with either event. Getting up early
is an incredible drag, or at least I should think it would be.

I would just like to point out that my pillow leaks feathers all
over me. I always look like a tax collector who has just been run
out of some rural community, probably on a rail.

Think I may get a car with my future writing money. Hate to
sell out to materialism, but I'm happy in a car. Just driving,
moving, rolling, streaming from one place. Not so much to
someplace. But from somewhere, going away, being in between,
going. Driving fast when certain songs are on. Sharing the road
with other cars and wondering who's in them and where they're
going. Parking is the antithesis of all this. I hate parking a car.

I walked about today. What happened to Manhattan should
not happen to any island. Not to say that New York is all bad.
It's mostly bad, but there are some good things. Central Park
for instance. Central Park is one of the better places in the
world. People don't go there specifically to be happy. They just
go there. And once there they don't have anything particular
to do, nowhere to hurry to go, and so they'll talk to you.

In the night I heard a radio discussion on Columbia. Judith
Crist blamed the whole thing on "balmy spring nights." Said
we "might as well be swallowing goldfish," which is untrue.

Another panelist said that a small hard-core group planned
the action a year ago, which would be a lie, except that the guy
believed it.

The moderator told an anecdote about a demonstrator with

a sign reading "Down with Everything That's Up," and said that what we (oldies) are doing today is paying the penalty for years of permissiveness, which is true, if permissiveness means raising kids to think and not obey any authority that happens to come stomping along.

All concurred that we students "should be busy studying to be leaders instead of carping about things."

Tuesday, June 25: A girl called who had seen me on the tube. She sounded beautiful, so I assumed she wasn't.

She was. Long dark hair. Tall. Thin. Big almond eyes. Beautiful this. Beautiful that. I couldn't believe her.

A friend called me and I told him about the girl. He then called back and told me that he and his brother felt that she was a federal agent. I thought that was incredible, but then I also thought it would be incredible if she weren't a fed. "But look," I said, "there are too many flaming subversives at Columbia for the authorities to bother with me." "Yeah, but you're the one who's been *writing*," he said. I locked the door before going to bed.

Wednesday, June 26: Ate dinner with Archibald Cox, ex-Solicitor General of the United States and Chairman of the Fact-Finding Commission. He said the law is like anything else. It can be used for good or for bad. He also ingested food and breathed, and I liked him. I couldn't help it.

Just heard an obnoxious ad (a redundant statement) for Nehru suits. If you find a good way to live or just something that you like, they take it and buy and sell it and never know what it's worth, and make it worth nothing. You turn to the East, and you end up with "guru-vy Gimbels."

I can look forward to little things. Right now I'm looking forward to brushing my teeth with a brand-new tube of toothpaste I bought. The trick is not to think about how someday it inevitably will be bent and twisted up with hard, dry paste at the end. Live for the moment, man.

Thursday, June 27: I don't understand why our government has us fight the war. I don't know. Are they incredibly evil men, or are they stupid, or are they insane? How can Johnson sleep? How can he go to bed knowing that 25,000 American boys—and countless Vietnamese—have died because of his "policies." He obviously doesn't consider the Vietnamese to be people at all. They're strange, distant, numberless, and yellow, so perhaps he can't empathize with them, can't know their existence and their joys. But what about the Americans? He thinks perhaps that the war is not going well. Doesn't he realize that wars can't go well, that people always die in them and that's not well? Doesn't he know anything? Do statistics hide the truth and keep him from feeling? When I see statistics I practically throw up. I can never forget it. It's in me that my friends everyday hear gunfire and see others fall and hate the enemy. But when they see the ground spin up at them and feel the wetness of their own blood, whom do you think they hate then? These kids who were and were being and were going to be, suddenly finding that they will not be what they wanted or anything else, suddenly finding themselves ending. Won't know or do anything any more. Never see or be seen again. Whom do you suppose they hate? Don't the leaders know that? Couldn't they work out a better way to settle problems? Little boys fight, but by the age of *sixteen*, as irresponsible teens, *they* see that fighting doesn't prove anything. Young men hardly ever fight. Only when their countries do. So it's the countries which display incredibly juvenile behavior. Wars are silly. They're ludicrous. But they're real, extant, constant, present. Why don't countries just stop it? Just cut it out, that's all. We don't want any. They struggle tortuously to arrive at disarmament pacts. They tell everybody that arriving at peace is complex, difficult. Don't they see? It's not a question of state department negotiations or of treaties or international law. It's very simple. All that's necessary is for the leaders to see what they've always done and are doing and for once know and feel and get sick and stop. Nobody fight any more. Of course it's not that simple. But I must be stupid because it seems that simple to me.

It seems that simple to me, and that's not a generation gap, it's an idea difference, and a power gap. You've got the power. You make millions of people suffer. They're hungry and they've got nowhere to go and nothing to do for it. Well cut it out, will you? Just stop it.

If you won't stop it we'll stop you. I've got nothing to lose. You can have your cars and your hi-fi's and your pools and your nice schools. (Sometimes.) I'd like to pawn them off and use the money for schools and houses for the poor. I'd like to do that so I'd feel good. So I'd feel good.

Let's not put our country down. It happens that the United States is the scourge of the earth, but let's not put it down.

I have a mad desire to live.

Hey, do you know what Communists do? They fall in love and have babies sometimes. I swear to God.

Friday, June 28: I think maybe I just did something I wasn't supposed to do. Something that isn't allowed. I just went away. Left things no one can leave. Laura and I went to the top of the Empire State Building during a thunderstorm. We went to live in the clouds.

I'm not there any more, but I can't come back. I must have made some kind of mistake and got lost. Now I'm caught in between.

I don't know how this can end.

I saw lightning. I heard it work. Who has stood beside lightning? I looked down into the measureless mists and shouted "Hey, New York! How does it feel to be down there when I'm up here?"

Isn't it singular that no one ever goes to jail for waging wars, let alone advocating them? But the jails are filled with those who want peace. Not to kill is to be a criminal. They put you right into jail if all you do is ask them to leave you alone. Exercising the right to live is a violation of law. It strikes me as quite singular.

Saturday, June 29: (At this point I fell in love, so the Book changes a bit. I didn't sing, and I didn't dance either, but I whistled a little and ran all the way home.)

I thought about dying today. I hadn't thought about it for quite some time. I usually spend about ten minutes a week thinking about it, but lately I just haven't put in any time thinking about dying.

I also took a cab today, at five in the morning.

"Do you want me to turn up Fourteenth Street?" the driver asked, prosaically enough.

"No. The corner's all right."

"No, really, your wish is my command."

I asked him if you have to be twenty-one to drive a cab, because I would like to drive a cab.

"Yeah," he answered. "Ever go to jail for a felony?"

"Misdemeanor."

"Just have to state it on your record. Of course you have to be nuts in the head."

"Oh, I've got that."

"Then you qualify."

All of this was in bringing Laura (who is the girl) home, where I told her about how I might disappear into the hills, come out to be named Pope, and then go back into the hills.

"Then you could send all the people back at the Vatican picture postcards every so often," she said.

"From Miami and Las Vegas."

"From Grossinger's."

I then went home, but not without meeting Miss Crush at the bus stop. She was standing there, officially pretty, with a little medal on the cap of her white uniform which read "Miss Crush." I thought I had stumbled upon Miss Orange Crush of 1968.

"What does 'Miss Crush' mean?" I asked.

"It's my name."

"Are you a stewardess?"

"Yes."

"Who for?"

"United."

"That's the biggest airline in the world," I said, making conversation.

"Yes. How did you know?" asked Miss Crush, feigning genuine interest.

"I've been on it. Read the little book. It says United flies about sixty zillion people every year and about twenty zillion every day. Do people ever get sick these days?"

She told me about three instances when people threw up.

Quite some time ago, many years ago in fact, before anybody was born, a seed drifted quietly down from a branch and was buried in the ground, where it grew. It grew into a tall tree, standing in the company of a forest in a land so green it was named "Green Land." No person ever came near, which was all right by the tree. Very recently, yesterday, if you want to know, a jet flew screaming by, unheard by the tree and, unseen by the tree, sprayed the air with poison which drifted quietly down and landed on the tree and, unfelt by the tree, killed the tree. This happens quite frequently, with the result that many trees die and the land is not green any longer. Where there was quiet life there is now violent death, which is why no one is concerned about the tree. There are too many men dying to worry about a tree. Or about a man.

· · ·

Sunday, June 30: Braving cultural shock, I went out to *suburbia* to spend the day at the *pool* at the *club* with Bill.

"Bill," I said. "The Book is shot. It's all over, Baby Blue."

"What do you mean?" (Bill had no way of knowing what I meant.)

I explained. "I haven't done *anything* in the last six days. I'm spending about ten hours a day with this girl Laura."

"You're going to blow the coin?" he asked, incredulously. "You don't have to if you don't want to."

"It doesn't have anything to do with what I want. It's just a description of reality. That's the way it *is*."

"God," Bill was sighing. "You're the biggest determinist."

"Hey! Let's grab the Skol, hit the sun, and Skol up a tan," I suggested.

We took it with us, but didn't put it on. We thought it sufficient that we had given it consideration and had it with us. Then Bill put some on. He agreed that it didn't do anything, but he didn't care about *having* it on. He liked *putting* it on. "Frottage," he explained happily.

I decided to put it on my right side only, to see if it made any difference. I got it in my eye.

"Don't put any in your other eye and see if it makes any difference"—Bill's idea.

It made no difference at all, to my eyes or my skin. No difference.

"Great stuff," we decided.

We talked about the art of walking down the sidewalk of Forty-sixth at Park, where Bill works, during lunch hour. I expressed my concern for the little old ladies who get blocked out and thrown in the gutter and all.

"Jeem," said Bill, "if they can't keep up with the pace, they should get out of the City."

I went home to my apartment and my roaches.

The roaches are a bit of a problem. We each have our areas. I have my corner, and they have the rest of the apartment. Except they always come into my corner.

Actually, the parallels between my roaches and the Viet Cong can hardly be ignored. There are seventeen parallels. Both my roaches and the V.C. are indigenous forces, are ignorant, ill-clad and underfed; they both drag away the bodies of their slain, come back no matter how many are killed, move by night, avoid prolonged engagements with the enemy, are not white, are fighting against people who are, have been fighting for generations, are of uncertain numbers, move via infiltration routes, are wily, are out-armed by the enemy, are contemptuous of death, are independent of outside control, are inscrutable, and are winning.

Before going to bed, I read a little more of Galbraith's *New Industrial State*, which is not bad, for a book.

Monday, July 1: Laura said whimsically, "You know, after we take over and rule the world, we've got to find out who *They* are."

"Then," I said, "we'll be *They*."

It occurred to me today, in a great flash of trying to think of something to write, that we could become a great country. What an opportunity! The field's wide open. There aren't any good countries. They're all bad, in varying degrees. We could become the first good country ever.

There used to be a dream for America. You know, the American dream? America was going to be different. Free. Good. Free and good. Of course they blew it right away. As soon as the Puritans came over they set up religious laws. But at least they clung to the dream. Until now. Now no one hopes for America to be different. I guess it was the dream that ruined the dream. People became convinced it was true, so they never made it true. People think the U.S.A. (a great-sounding, nice, informal name) is special, so we can do anything and it's okay (an American expression). People should wake up and dream again.

. . .

Tuesday, July 2: I went to open a savings account at the Banker's Trust. On a bus that morning I'd seen an ad which said "You'll find a banker at Banker's Trust." Something about that statement intrigued me and I decided on the spot that that had to be my bank.

Arriving at the bank I noted a poster in the window which asserted that "You'll find a banker at Banker's Trust." Inside I was taken care of by a Mr. McNamara who shook my hand and assured me that "You'll find a banker at Banker's Trust."

"Yeah, I know," I said.

He was, being a banker, somewhat wary of my check. But he cashed it. He said that he hoped by risking a favor for me, he'd get me to do business with him in the future. *Do business.* What a groove. I've never done business with anyone before.

That's not quite true. I've been a customer. I remember I got a letter from Eastern Airlines last winter. "Good news, Mr. Kunen!" it began. "On Thursday, February 15, the entire Eastern Air Shuttle system goes jet-powered." I remember it because we all went over to the West End to celebrate. (The West End is a pretentious collegiate bar where pretentious collegiate people go to act pretentious, at no little expense.)

Post-bank I went with Laura to the home of her friend who was going to Europe. Le grand tour.

There a cat scratched me, which prompted me to say, "I hope they heal into long white scars. Then maybe people will think I belong to a dueling society." As we left I said, "I'll carry your books. Then maybe people will think I'm a scholar." (I seem to be concerned about what people will think.)

Outside. "What kind of car's that?" asked Laura's friend, pointing to a phallic extension at the curb.

"That's a Maserati overhead balls super-hemi." I was irritated. Talking about Columbia, the child of affluence had said, "There's no excuse for *vandalism*, but you had a right to *riot.*"

. . .

Thursday, July 4: I am going summer home to Hyannis for the weekend to write the entire book. Aside from the fact that I have no money, I want to hitchhike anyway. Hitchhiking is a way to look for America. Gallup takes polls; I take rides to find out where people are at.

I made a graphic-artsy sign to try to convey to the motoring public that I am an interesting person. In the corner I drew an American flag as a concession to the holiday. Also, I hope it may soften the effects of my hair somewhat. As a rule, hitchhiking travel time is directly proportional to the length of your hair.

No sooner did I hit the road than a 1200c.c. dynamatic Harley-Davidson mammoth motorcycle approached me, with an officer of the law astride it. I considered making a break for it, but realized that would be an admission that I was doing something illegal, which is always a good thing to avoid, especially when you *are* doing something illegal. He didn't savagely beat me, but told me that hitching was prohibited on state roads *and* anywhere within New York City—double damning me. What should I do then, I wanted to know. He was of the opinion that that was my problem, which I suppose it was.

He left and I moved and I was picked up and I left. But the ride (two teen girls who were probably on their way to pick up a carton of Coke) only took me to New Rochelle. As I stood on the side of the road my thoughts centered around the prospect of the "Pokey"—where a state trooper had once threatened to put me when he caught me hitching at 3 A.M.

But the president-elect of the New Rochelle High School student government finally arrived and thought he knew me from somewhere. As he was moving me ten miles I explained that he'd seen me on the tube, and he explained how things were at New Rochelle. He'd raised one hundred sixty-five bills to buy an anti-war ad in the school paper, and then the principal, who is widely held to be a bad person, refused to let the ad run. The paper, the principal said, must not be used for political ends, although he didn't say why. The students said "repression"

—at that word, the American Civil Liberties Union came in. The left people threatened to walk out of the graduation exercises, which presumably would have embarrassed the principal. Meanwhile certain teachers were allegedly calling up football team members suggesting they pound the crap out of anybody who might spoil the commencement. The principal would not take any steps to protect the dissenting ones from this threat, but rather began selective enforcement of little school rules to harass the activists. Eventually a compromise was reached that was equally unsatisfactory to everybody, thus avoiding the walk-out.

I found all of this very interesting, because there seemed to be valid issues involved, some of them even relevant to education. (One complaint was that students could no longer get together and ask to be taught a course in anything they wanted, as they once had.) I had heard on the radio that kids were jumping around for no earthly reason at all at New Rochelle. I invited the kid to drop by the Liberation School and we parted friends.

Five rides and two hours later I was still nowhere. If you're ever hitchhiking, arrange not to be left off at Danny's Diner near Milford, Connecticut, because you'll *never* get out. You wouldn't believe the quality of the traffic there—all middle-aged, all couples, all on their way home to relax with the *Reader's Digest*. I was finally picked up by a Boston University business student who was smoking grass as he drove. He maintained that "It's the only way to drive," but he had a tendency to get in the way of other cars, and I was almost glad when he dropped me off.

Then a hippy-ish couple took me. The girl offered me a slice of watermelon. When I was through with it she urged me to throw the rind out the window—inciting to litter. Just what I needed—get busted for a littering rap on top of six counts of hitchhiking with long hair. I avoided arrest, however, and they dropped me off in East Haven. "Have a good marriage," I said, as they had told me they were getting married.

I stood at the side of the road in East Haven for a terribly long time. I began to hallucinate, but not really—I remembered the date and realized it was fireworks I was seeing. Must have been 8:30 at least.

Soon it would be completely dark. I considered crossing over to the other side of the highway and trying to get back to New Haven for a bus. But that would be an incredible cop out. Besides, my magic ride might be on the way. If I quit now, think of the people I might have met but will never meet.

For the love of God, I said, somebody pick me up. But then I've got Laura, I can't ask for anything else. All right, but if it's all the same to You, *let* somebody pick me up without divine intervention.

A couple of times guys in cars gave me the finger. My reaction to that is generally one of relief that they didn't throw anything at me. Then a car came by and threw a beer can at me.

Then Wally and Jack stopped by. Wally and Jack were two high school grads returning to Fall River from a celebratory trip to New York. We immediately had to change a tire. That left one decent tire and three bald. Wally kept to around forty-five though, which is considerably faster than standing on the side of the road, so I was very happy.

But when we neared Fall River Wally hit ninety and I could smell the tire rubber burning. Okay, I asked myself—now, now are you sorry you hitched? When we crash, *then* I'll be sorry. Buses tip over, trains collide, planes fall down. (Ships sink.)

We didn't crash. It was midnight when they dropped me at the Fall River Bus Terminal. It was closed. I called my Fall River friend to find that there was no one home.

Fall River is an interesting city. It is a great cotton mill center from which all the cotton mills moved fifty years ago. It's quite a tough place to be in in the nighttime.

I thought about calling home, because my parents had been expecting me during the day. But what could I say: "Hi Mom, I'm stranded in Fall River, with two dollars and nowhere to go. I'll try not to freeze to death and maybe I'll see you tomorrow."

I had resigned myself to being mugged when I brought myself up short. "Mugged, mugged, you're always going to be mugged. Did you ever consider getting knifed?"

I got back on the road and by 1 A.M. got one of those little rides that take you from somewhere to nowhere. At nowhere I stood and sat as a cold fog set in and it became 2 A.M. and then three.

I stood by a red light where people had a good chance to look me over. They would point at me and talk about me and drive away.

Please, please, please pick me up. What stories I could tell you. I could relate tales of Columbia to make your blood run cold. C'mon, pick me up somebody please I'm cold and I've nowhere to go can't you see that?

I threw myself at the mercy of the American people and was rebuffed completely.

I started singing "We shall not be moved." A guy came by with greased hair and a T-shirt and offered to take me half a mile to the bowling alley. I thought I'd be better off staying at the intersection. He said "Okay, Peace," by which I thought he meant "Good luck fella," but then he gave the "V" and I gave it back saying "We will man," and knew it to be true. That was the trip for me.

But for all that I grew colder and cursed myself for forgetting that bowling alleys are invariably characterized by four walls and a roof.

A car slowed to a stop and when I moved to it, it sped off, the people inside laughing. That made me sad. I mean really if they don't want to pick me up, fine, I could be a crook. But why, why do that to me?

A car came by with a fishing pole hanging out and I yelled, "Good! Have a fishing rod sticking out the window. See if I care!" When you start talking like that you know you're going to be all right, because you're at your lowest. I readjusted my nice leather bag to show as prominently as possible on the roadside. Look everybody, I'm affluent, for Christ's sake.

Then came Reggie Andre, a black man from Falmouth who

used to hitch all the time and can't stand to pass anybody up. I thanked him as much as I could short of saying I loved him, which might have been misconstrued. He bought me a cup of coffee, and not only was it a dime and good, but they refilled it free which is something I thought no longer existed. As we drove we talked about black power and the war and he was, I swear, much whiter than I am, which is good because if you accept the premise that blacks can be whiter than whites, then the whole color thing becomes quite confusing and maybe everyone will just forget about it.

He took me all the way to Falmouth, which is just fifteen miles through the woods from Hyannis. I was hoping he might say what the hell and take me home but that would have been a lot to ask. As he dropped me off in the blackness of night forest he said that I shouldn't have any trouble getting a ride there—lots of traffic. I thanked him again and swore he'd be in my book, which you see he is.

I decided to walk and was quite happy because it would be morning soon and I'd survived. The birds began to stir and I had them all to myself. I heard a hush and felt the gathering warm. The sun bobbed up from behind the edge of the world, into the bottom of the sky. "As the sun goes up over Cape Cod," I composed, "the gaseous ethery fog of morning drifts to the sky, and leaves the ground floor of Creation to Humanity." Also, "They rolled out the gray tar carpet for me, and I walked up it, and I walked down it and walked a long way on it, all the way home." I was quite giddy.

A summer kid milkman gave me a lift, and then some obnoxious rowdies, as it were, who wanted to know what could be expected from girls on the Cape, took me to my door, but not before I had walked six miles.

Friday, July 5, 6:30 A.M. Thirteen rides, thirteen hours. I felt the dawn walk was so beautiful it had made it all worth it. Something has to make it all worth it, and that's what I chose.

I creep into the house and go to sleep. Next my mother wakes

me. "I assume," I say, "that you have been somewhat concerned regarding my whereabouts."

Radio: "The American fighter pilot who made the kill said,
'I've waited all my life for this.' " Waited all his life to kill
someone. He said it took him about ninety seconds to fire the
air-to-air missile. Took him about ninety seconds to kill someone.

Saturday, July 6: I tell my mother that I've been looking for a
car to buy.

"I don't think you should buy a car," she says.

"Oh. Why not?"

"Because you've got just about enough money to pay for one
year of college."

"Oh," I said, beginning to comprehend.

"And if you get kicked out of Columbia, you're going to have
to pay for your own college."

"Oh, really," I said, thinking about what I was thinking. I
was thinking that it would be pretty exciting being on my own.
I could write and drive a cab part-time and get a loan and just
barely get by. The whole starving artist scene. And I was thinking
that was a silly thing to think.

I decided to leave. I said I was leaving because the house was
too full of people for me to get anything done, which was true,
but then I never get anything done under any circumstances.
I left really because of the hostility. When I first arrived hostility embraced me and wouldn't let go as long as I stayed. You
know—hair. They wanted me to get my hair cut.

Which leads me to write what I fervently hope will be the
last words anyone bothers to write on the subject in twentieth-
century American letters.

HAIR

Hairs are filamentous chains of living cells which grow out of
the epidermis. The very hairs of your head are all numbered
(St. Matthew 10:30), but their length is a function only of how

often they are cut—a matter of personal choice. Medical science has yet to discover any positive correlation between hair length and anything—intelligence, virility, morality, cavities, cancer—anything.

Long hair on men, however, has been known to make some people sick.

My father, for instance. On July 8, 1968, he alleged that long hair on his sons made him sick. "You look like a woman," he said. "I'll get a haircut," I said. That threw him off, but only for a moment. "If I were a girl," he continued, "I wouldn't like the way you look." "You are not a girl," I said, "and anyway, I said I'd get a haircut." "I don't see how your hair could possibly get any longer," he added. "Would you agree," I asked, "that if I let it grow for another two months, it would get longer?" "Maybe," he conceded, "but it just couldn't possibly be any longer."

My father talks about the bad associations people make when they see someone with hair. I come back with the bad associations people make when they see someone replete with a shiny new Cadillac that looks like it should have a silk-raimented coachman standing at each fender. But as for bad vibrations emanating from my follicles, I say great. I want the cops to sneer and the old ladies swear and the businessmen worry. I want everyone to see me and say "There goes an enemy of the state," because that's where I'm at, as we say in the Revolution biz.

Also, I like to have peace people wave me victory signs and I like to return them, and for that we've got to be able to recognize each other. And hair is an appropriate badge. Long hair should be associated with peace, because the first time American men wore short hair was after World War I, the first time great numbers of American men had been through the military.

Armies always shave hair to deprive the soldier of his individuality and his masculinity. (Yes, masculinity. Samson, much?) They want to depersonalize and humiliate you so that you aren't anybody any more and you'll have to prove yourself to them in their way, so that you have to develop new values, their values, and become a killer.

So if long hair just happens to be the peace thing, it's an appropriate happening.

I once read somewhere that older generatees who cast aspersions on the masculinity of hair people fear for their own masculinity.

Archibald Cox (crew-cut) told me that he thought anyone who made a big thing about kids' hair was loony as hell (or something to that effect. I don't remember his exact words).

Then there is the burn (side) question. "Are you going to let them grow or are you going to trim them?" my mother asked me in what I think was a tone of resigned curiosity. "I don't know," I said. "I haven't decided whether I want to emulate Martin Van Buren or Abraham Lincoln."

I lit out for the Marlboro home, in my mother's car, snatching up every hitch-hiker I could find. A couple were going to Boston, so I took them to Boston. When I finally neared Marlboro I decided to cruise for a while. I turned off onto a country road and cruised about for three hours, trying to stay in the woods. You can't do it. What I found out was that all roads lead to somewhere. You can't go to nowhere. The best you can do is not to care where you go and hope to end up at small places that you've never heard of. I just kept rolling around until the Boston stations started to fade and the road signs were talking about Rhode Island. Then I decided to head back, but not very purposefully. I figured I'd keep the setting sun on my left and maybe I'd come home, which I did. But then I cruised the Main Street six times deciding that Marlboro, with its 25,000 people, is indeed a City, as it claims. The cultural dividing line between a city and a town is hard to define, but I'd say a town is a place where if you see a kid with long hair, you can assume it's a girl.

I sought out and rolled by every place I had any images for—the grammar school, the streets I think I once had friends on back in the child-time, my street. Eventually the fuel needle fell below the big E and I surrendered to my house.

I saw my only friend in Marlboro, a guy named Willy, who lives next door. I asked him what's he been doing, fooling around? "Playing," he said, preferring its more respectable connotations. I gave him a wild flower I had raped from the woods, and with that he decided I was indeed weird. The man's only three years old, but his openness is closing already. He's beginning to know the players according to society's scorecard.

I went in and sat down and read nearly every word of a three-day-old paper. Then I watched a couple of old movies on the tube. Then I made phone calls, listened to the radio, read a two-day-old paper, went out and said hello to the stars and especially the Milky Way. It struck me that I had not devoted a moment's thought to the Milky Way in months. Hadn't considered it at all. Then I went in to work on the Book. It was 4 A.M. I had left Cape Cod at 1 P.M. I have a tendency to procrastinate.

The radio is on. You should listen to the radio because there's a chance you might hear "Sky Pilot" by The Animals. It's a song about a military clergyman. I thought I had heard Sky Pilot several times over the car radio. But I hadn't really, because it turns out the song is quite long and the real skinny is at the end—a controversial line: "Thou shalt not kill." They never play that part over the AM pop stations except safely into the empty air of night.

Sunday, July 7: The heading "July 7" is a concession to the hard-working ancient astronomers who calculated the calendar. I didn't go to bed, so for me Saturday-Sunday has been one million-dollar weekend lump.

At 5:30 the goddamn birds started waking up with their familiar cry of "Another-day-gone-and-you-haven't-done-shit caw,

caw, caw, jweep." I went outside to breathe some cold air and wake up, but figured I'd go for a spin in the auto. Spun around twenty miles looking for an open gas station.

It's God-day today. Everybody makes the worship scene for an hour and comes out feeling good. That's the trouble. They should come out feeling like doing good, but instead they feel good already without doing anything. I don't mean to put down everybody who goes to church. Some of my best friends go to church. But it does happen, for instance, that American church-goers as a group are more bigoted than those who deal with God in other ways.

Of course, certain religious individuals may drag down the group as a whole. George Wallace, for instance. He puts in his pray-time and then goes around urging people to vote for him so he can have "a crease put in the forehead" of everybody who demonstrates for peace or against poverty. Or take President Johnson. Sometimes he goes to church twice in one day, which shows a real religious commitment, because genocide is hard work, and he can't have much free time.

They call themselves Christians, the big men; they all go to church. I think that's a pretty bad joke. It's in poor taste and it isn't funny. Whom do they think they're fooling? Maybe they're fooling God. That's it. They must be. They must be fooling God.

This scene of going to church on Sunday and playing with the kids, then kissing the wife good-bye Monday morning and heading down to the office to work on maximizing kill-densities or something, is what Hanna Arendt refers to as the banality of evil. Specifically she talks about Adolph Eichmann. The man was not a screaming lunatic. He was a quiet upstanding civil servant who wouldn't kick a dog if it were biting him. But he had a job to do which his society called right and he did it. Much—very much—like Johnson, Rusk, McNamara, Hum-phrey, Westmoreland or the professor doing IDA research. None of them foam at the mouth (although they have been known to talk irrationally). They all lead healthy family lives, dull regular lives.

The Bio-warfare researcher arrives home at a little after six because the traffic was bad. He nods to the kids. "Hi, Johnny. Hi, Sue. What's for dinner, hon?"

"Pot roast. How's the deadly botulism contagion coming?"

"Not bad. Got a new man in today who thinks he can make it immune to boiling. Y'know, so they won't be able to drink no matter what."

"So it's botulism or thirst, right?"

"Uh huh. It's up to the enemy. Say, did somebody dent the car?"

Evil is a drag. The men don't wear black hats. Resistance to evil isn't terribly stirring either, on the left, I mean. It isn't one blood-boiling shoot-out with the cops after another, you know. The average leftist deals with cops when he wants to know directions and that's it. I'm thinking of writing a book called the *Banality of Everything*.

When I got back this morning from my gas expedition I agreed to let myself view just a little tube before I settled down to work. After watching a Catholic video mass I caught the end of "Milton the Monster," which dealt with inept motorcycle cops trying with consistent unsuccess to nab speeders and also violence. Then I got involved in "Leonard the Lion," which featured good grammar, big words, a substructure of adult humor, aerial strafing, and numerous dynamite blasts. That was followed by "Bugs Bunny," which offered several airplane crashes amid the gradual escalation of a dog vs. cat fight.

Post cereals sponsored and they had several beautifully photographed, expertly cut pieces for Alpha-bits which *starred* a little black girl. Suburban, to be sure, but black nonetheless.

M&M's still melt in the same place—it's nice to know that some things are constant—but one bag had somehow come into the possession of a young black. I was very happy to see these ads. I suppose the motivation behind them is to convince the black community not to burn down the M&M factory, which makes it tokenism and co-option, but the fact remains that all of the nation's future whites are watching these ads.

In the afternoon, after taking in the first game of a Red Sox doubleheader via the tube, I decide to attend the second in the flesh. It's a sellout, but I have no trouble parking because I know a spot for thirty cars that only twenty-nine other people in the world know about. Getting in the park was a different story, in which there is a lesson.

I arrive with epauletted gray shirt, worn dungarees, disheveled long hair, rectangular wire shades and, lest there be any doubt, the notorious name "Columbia" emblazoned across my chest. There are no more tickets. "Is there any way I can get into the ball park?" I ask desperately. The turnstile attendant thinks it might help me if I went for a little walk (the cops watch him, while other cops watch the cops) and then returned to him with a deuce in my hand. I do that and he lets me in. He probably thought I was a peacenik intellectual disloyal commie, but if so I was a peacenik intellectual disloyal commie with two dollars for him, and that's what counts. Money is ideologically pure. It sullies everyone equally and therefore can't be sullied by anyone. Radicals: your coin is as good as anybody else's. "Money talks, nobody walks," whatever it may mean, is true.

Inside the park there were 35,000 people, a great many of them staring at me. I just wanted to come and watch a ball game, but once your appearance tips off where you're at, every move you make is political. I didn't think I would be the only 'nik there. And if I was, I didn't see why people should mind. But it seemed that they were saying "Get out. This is our place. We don't want to be reminded of politics or peace here. This is not the place. We are here for baseball."

I was there for baseball too. But I couldn't enjoy it. I couldn't enjoy it probably because people were staring at me, or because I thought people were staring at me. But perhaps I couldn't enjoy it because of the war. How can you care about baseball while the war goes on?

But you should care about baseball, because baseball is something you like, damn it. You can't stop the war by giving up baseball. In fact, I think all 35,000 people at the game were giving a massive demonstration for peace whether they knew it or not and whether they would have wanted to or not. Going to a game is a peace demonstration and going to the beach is a war protest and the movies are Vietnam rallies because they're all cases of people doing something they like and enjoying themselves and not hurting anybody. Everybody who roots for a team is saying this is important to me. They are doing what is important to them. Doing what you like, what you know is unimportant but what you damn well like is being free and happy just a little and it's very opposite to fighting wars.

But if you care about the Boston Red Sox too much you can forget about other things that shouldn't be forgotten. At any bar in Boston you will hear men fervently discussing Yastremski's slump to the exclusion of starvation and death which must be stopped before Yaz's next home run can truly be cause for joy.

In the pennant year of 1967 I used to say that the Red Sox stood for all that's good in the world—happiness, enthusiasm, courage. Then I began to say they *were* all that's good in the world. Because of them I could talk to anybody at all and share something and be together and understand. They were very important in that way. They were something people would open to you for.

But I tried to go back this year and it's a year later. I was apart from the crowd and I couldn't come home to it.

Monday, July 8: Back at Columbia I went to a class at the Strike Committee's Summer Liberation School. I didn't really listen, but there was a pretty good fan in the room and I thought some.

There was one oldish man in the class who features "hierarchical society" and manages to talk about it no matter what the subject is supposed to be.

He says everybody, including movement people, is completely

hung up with status. That kind of hit home with this boy, because I've been angling for a position as Lord High Propagandist or something, so that I'd have a place and a role and feel comfortable in the shadow of the valley of Revolution.

Two good ideas of his: Do away with "post no bills" signs so people could put up their ideas on walls, and likewise make a page in every newspaper available for anybody to write anything he wants, not subject to the selection of the editors.

This ego-blast book I'm writing fits well into the anti-hierarchy scheme, it seems to me, because I am not an author, nor will I be an author once having written a book. This seems altogether fitting and also proper. Why should only book writers write books? Who cares about them? They're not where it's at. Let everybody write so that no one is a writer.

Tuesday, July 9: America. Listen to it. *America.* I love the sound. I love what it could mean. I hate what it is.

I was looking through the July 1 issue of *Rat* today. I read how the narcs came and busted Jerry Rubin, a founder of the Yippies. They busted him on pot possession; they busted him because he doesn't like the way things are and he's spreading the word and working against the system and even has pictures of Castro around. They tore apart his apartment and also beat him up, rupturing a disk in his back. I don't know Rubin but I do know narcs and I can't stand them, the ugly Fascist brute pigs. Goddamn and just assume I'm listing a lot of foul obscenities.

In America you shouldn't have to worry about police busting into your apartment and beating you up. I specifically remember seeing a TV show around thirteen years ago about an immigrant couple who still had their old country fears and thought the mailman was a cop coming to take them away. They weren't confused; they were just ahead of their time.

It makes me feel quite sad. I mean, I'm an American, and look what my country is doing. And I can't seem to do a thing about it; me, or anybody else. We've gone into the streets, and we've gone to Washington, to the Pentagon, and what good does it do? You work in politics and you win the people to your side, and what good does that do? I'm about ready to give up.

Wednesday, July 10: Weather good today. Wind west-southwest, steady at ten knots. Held course. Man overboard trying to hoist jib sheet. Sighted land. Flying fish all day. Nothing to report.

Thursday, July 11: If a country has to draft men to defend it, then there is nothing to defend. If there is something to defend, but a draft is still necessary, then the nation's defense is not in question.

Friday, July 12: Laura has decided to go to Canada to check out the draft refusers there—to be better informed for her Resistance work. Laura works for the Resistance. She's about as radical as you can be without wanting to hurt people. She's also a women's liberationist. She wears eye makeup, Paraphernalia clothes and a red armband. She's very feminine.

I figure I might as well go too. I'll get some stuff for the Book. I envision interviewing seething exile after seething exile, finding out what (or if) they think of Columbia and the Clean One, and how it feels to be turfless, and why they chose Canada over prison and if they want to come back.

We borrowed a car of my cousin's, a Daf, a Dutch shopping cart, mounted with a two-cylinder lawnmower engine, that can do fifty-five downhill with a good wind.

We drove for hours and then hours more, and though we moved a little better after I smelled something burning and released the parking brake, I considered the "80" on the speedometer a cruel joke perpetrated by the automotive Biggees of the Netherlands. That car might reach eighty if it were dropped from a plane.

After eight hours and 400 miles had passed beneath our wheels, we were in Montreal. We headed for McGill and asked hairs there where the Resistance office was. They didn't know but directed us to an organization called Contact, "a sort of help for needy hippies place." As we walked up the steps a neighbor said "Here come two more kids looking for a place to crash."

Inside a girl combed her files trying to find out for us where the Resistance was. She was interrupted when two kids came in looking for a place to crash, but she ultimately found the address. I was a little ashamed of not being what we seemed to be.

We went straight to the headquarters—there was no point stopping to eat because we had no money for food. When we arrived the Resistance guys were just starting a meeting and they suggested we come back later, but we said, "Ten minutes, we've come from New York," and they said "All right, we'll rap to you and then have our meeting."

"Is it true that it's really hard to get work here?"

"No. It's easy."

"How about a place to live?"

"No problem."

"Well, where could we go to talk to some kids? Where do they hang out?"

"They don't hang out. They all go their separate ways and live all over and just want to forget all about the U.S. and the draft. They weren't political back in the States and they're not political here. The political ones are more in prison. These kids just didn't want to go to Vietnam so they came up here and that's that. They grew up in suburbia and they come here and find a very American culture that they feel comfortable with."

The boy explaining all this spoke in the quiet, precise, tired, patient voice characteristic of people in the movement. I don't know why it's characteristic of the movement to speak quietly, precisely, tiredly and patiently, but it is.

There was one kid we might see, a Gerry Bornstein who was trying to organize an American in Exile political force but had only about twelve followers. He was trying to publish a mag called *The Rebel* but it had come out only twice. We bought the two issues and took his address and also the address of a place called Logos where we might find Americans and thanked them very much and went out.

In the car I suggested we go to Toronto because Montreal obviously wasn't where it was at. Laura said "Sure, let's go." I said "Don't fantasy around with me because I'll take you up on it and I'll really go." (I felt too sick and tired to look up Bornstein or Logos or even sleep in the car. All I could conceive of doing was letting a motor pull my passive body along the roads of Canada.) She said she was quite capable of as much absurdity as I was and she was actually willing to go.

So we went to a gas station and asked which road to Toronto, which is exactly analogous to pulling up to a pump in New York and saying "Excuse me, but could you please direct me to Detroit."

Directed, we set out, but first we thought we'd buy a loaf of bread to feed on over the next two days. We went to a lot of markets that had meat and dead fish lying around. They smelled very strongly of the fact that here was food. I can't say I liked the smell but it was at least natural, very different from the sterile food distribution center that is the American supermarket. The thing was that it being ten at night the stores were out of bread. In looking for bread we made a startling discovery. We found perhaps the only corner of the continent and maybe the world which is not subject to the sway of American capitalist hegemony. THE WEST END MEAT MARKET in Montreal, Quebec, Canada, will not accept American money. Period. No American coin for that man. He may know something we don't know. Laura didn't care. She doesn't eat meat anyway. She empathizes with animals.

We finally found a place where we were given the bread free plus thirty-three cents. We gave the shopkeeper our $10 American bill, and in return he gave us the bread and $10.33 Canadian money. We referred to the Canadian coin as play money and therefore didn't mind seeing it dwindle away. It seemed extraordinarily fortunate that people were willing to accept it at all, so we might as well spend it while we could.

We asked a French cop to give us directions to Toronto and

he seemed pleased to help us. Maybe I was projecting, but he really did seem pleased.

We stopped at a gas station and while the tank was being filled Laura disappeared. I asked the attendant kid where she might be and he said he didn't know, that there were a lot of dirty old men around the station. I asked if I was talking to one of them and he laughed. We joked around and he explained to me how imperial gallons are bigger than American gallons. His friend came over and admired the car, saying he was Dutch and loved everything Dutch. That's a nice thing. Imagine if you could be American and love everything American.

Laura came back. She'd been talking to the owner of the station. She always talks to strangers. He'd asked what we were doing and she'd said to herself damn it, she's going to tell anyone exactly what we're doing, and she told him about working for the Resistance. She was very pleased that he didn't bat an eyelash, didn't see anything wrong with being a 'nik at all.

Then we set out on our 360-mile jaunt trek to Toronto. I remembered reading that there was grass planted by hitch-hikers all along the Trans-Canada Highway, but we soon forked off it to Route 401. Laura said that she felt like she was a hitch-hiker and I'd just picked her up. (Laura often has metaphorical feelings.)

I told her we were on an allegorical journey, a mystical trip that really had nothing to do with Montreal or Toronto. What we were doing was going to places together. Right then we passed a sign which said entering Future, I swear to God.

Those highways are boring enough in the daytime but at night, at night you are just sitting still, vibrating slightly, as a film loop of flashing white dashes is projected incessantly before you.

At about 4 A.M. the darkness parted on our left to reveal the glitter of a vast moonlit expanse of water. The water went on and on and on like the ocean but no waves. My God, it's a Great Lake, I said. What a great lake. We stopped and stood on the shore. This, we ruled, made the entire trip worth it.

. . .

Saturday, July 13: We had come 180 miles to Kingston and we slept in the car there.

The next morning Laura was telling me that I had a cold and for the sake of my health she swore it we should head back to New York. She pleaded with me, not realizing that I *might* have gone on to Toronto at gun point.

So, having spent ten minutes delving into the exile situation in Canada, we headed home. We hadn't had a meal in a day and we had maybe enough money for gas back to the city if we avoided paying any tolls.

As a last resort we hoped we could barter cigarettes for fuel.

We went over a suspension bridge into the U.S. It was one of those with a metal grate roadway. If you stick your head out the window and look straight down it looks like you're suspended in air a hundred feet over the river. That also helped make the trip worth it.

We told the toll collector we had no money so he took our address for billing without much hassle.

Canadian customs waved us through but the bored civil servants at the American customs office had been waiting for us all day, maybe all year.

We had to pull over and go in. He asked me who owned the car and then quick where does he live. I knew where he lived.

Does your cousin know you have his car? I wanted to say, "In the broadest sense, does anyone know who has his car?" But I didn't and we were on our way.

Canadians are nicer than Americans, or at least they're nicer to Americans than Americans are.

As we moved south gas stations accepted our play money with increasing reluctance and markdown or markup or whatever you call it.

We finally reached the environs of New York with little gas and no money (actually one cent, but it was a gray one and I didn't want to spend it). We lost our way and stopped to ask a man for directions into Manhattan. He said that he had just arrived from Toronto himself and had looked for three hours for a place to stay. He chatted, patting my arm, and gave us good directions.

"Canadians," said Laura.

"Yeah," I agreed. "Canadians."

We drove into the city via the toll station exact change booth, into which we threw no exact change.

Sunday, July 14: Relating events becomes difficult when there are no events to relate.

Monday, July 15: I went downtown to try to get my tape recorder repaired, trying not to get a parking ticket while I was at it. I failed in both endeavors.

"This is a pretty old machine," said the man in the service department.

The thing's six years old. If it were a kid it'd be in the first grade. But you're not supposed to have bought a tape recorder that long ago, and if you did, you're not supposed to have kept it.

So the man couldn't fix the microphone, but he sold me a plug for $1.50. *One dollar and fifty cents.* I would have been able to go to the movies six times for that when I was a kid.

July 15, 1972: The young man walks into a restaurant. "I'll have a cheeseburger," he says. "How much?"

Says the counterman: "That's $8.00 and $1.60 tax makes $9.60."

"How do you sell them so cheap?"

"Volume."

"Well, here's a $500 bill and let's see if I have the 60 cents. Nope, all my change rusted again."

Back at the apartment I read a mimeographed paper by Tony Papert called *The Mass Strike*. It began:

The coincidence of Columbia and Paris should dispel the dominant illusion of the left in this country: That our radicalism is derived

mainly from the particular issues of the Viet Nam war and racism
... In fact, our Viet Nam and racism issues are only particular manifestations of far deeper forces simultaneously energizing mass actions
in diverse parts of the advanced capitalist sector.

That may not be terribly surprising, but it hit me kind of hard.
Like it dispelled my dominant illusion.

(We youths say "like" all the time because we mistrust reality.
It takes a certain commitment to say something *is*. Inserting
"like" gives you a bit more running room.)

I've never been much of a political comprehension man. I'm
more of an issue man. I don't know much about the capitalist
sector, but I know what I like, and I don't like the Nam war or
racism. Papers like *The Mass Strike* just don't speak to me right
now.

But I thought that Papert might, so I went to see him in the
evening. We went to a bar and talked over the bourgeois blare
of a Jerry Lewis movie on the decadent color TV on the wall.

Papert is head of the SDS Labor Committee. The Labor Committee is sometimes referred to as the thought faction, as opposed to the action faction, of SDS. I thought I might pick up a
few thoughts.

I asked him, with some embarrassment over the incredible
simplicity of my political consciousness, what difference it makes
who the Trustees are.

He said it's not important who they are; it's what they do.
What they do is use the University to shape, train, and funnel
manpower, for the needs of the American capitalist empire.

I asked him if he thought we'd made any mistakes in the
strike.

He thought we'd taken a political step backward by organizing
on a constituency basis. Students should play an important role
in the revolutionary process, yet we have students concentrating
on student gripes, letting blacks worry about blacks, women
take care of women, laborers labor, and so on.

Essentially what he said was that everybody's got to be together in a big thing. Local organizing around parochial issues
is not the way. The first proper step is to educate everybody to
the fact that what's putting them down is the capitalist system.
The Labor Committee was currently leafleting garment workers.

I asked him whom he wanted to be the next President of the
country. I wanted to know if it was possible for me to be a decent
radical and still root for Clean.

He said liberals like McCarthy are concerned with co-opting
militants, especially black nationalists. That's what local control
is about: the classic Fascist method of destroying a movement
by isolating little groups to deal with the top. That way you give
them the traffic light or the textbook they want, but never
freedom. Therefore, it would be better for the movement if "one
of the flunkies," Humper or the Dick, were elected. Then there
wouldn't be any co-opting sops thrown to the people, and the
Revolution could go on developing.

It seemed to me that he was essentially saying that people
should be kept unhappy so that they will know they're unhappy.
They mustn't be fooled by improvement of things. I agree that
Clean tries to co-opt people with little things, but if they're a
little happier for it, I'm for it. Let the liberals do their little re-
forms and if they're really meaningless sops, the people will
decide that and keep pushing.

I asked Tony if he would do *anything* to build the Revolution,
and he said that he would.

Then we talked about gun control laws.

He, like all the real radicals, was against gun control legislation. He pointed out, correctly, that with the new laws, eighty
percent of the blacks would not be able to get guns. Also leftists
couldn't get them whereas all the flaming Birchers and suburban
reactionaries would be armed to the teeth. He said the Constitution guaranteed the right to bear arms in order to counterpose an
armed populace to the armed state. That's true. And he said real
gun control isn't possible until you disarm the police. I agree but

the police aren't about to be disarmed, certainly not while other people have guns. He said the real point of the legislation is to prevent the blacks from defending themselves against the cops who shoot them every day. I wonder, if that's true, why Wallace and Southern senators are against gun control? Anyway, if the blacks get armed, the police will just use it as an excuse for more shooting, and in shoot-outs the state always wins. They'll bomb out blocks in Harlem if they want to.

I just don't like guns. I don't want anybody to have them. People who talk about this or that group being better armed than another are talking as if they were playing some sort of game where you move gun pieces around to best advantage. They couldn't realize that in real life you don't draw a card that says "dead," you feel bullets tearing into you and breaking your bones and leaving holes out of which all your blood runs as you lie in the gutter dying. I don't want that to happen to any person, including persons who for good or bad or no reasons are cops. There must be better ways to fight guns than with guns, and if there aren't we ought to think up some. If we get guns we're just like them and have no right or reason to fight them and everybody would be better off without us.

Tuesday, July 16: Right now I'm not in favor of a Revolution, but only for the same reason I'm against writing the Book or going to Liberation classes. They all take energy, and it's 96° in the big city. There are times when ideology has to bow to meteorology.

A song came on the radio, The Rascals' "People've Got to be Free." And it hit me, what the hell does it mean. Free? Free to do what? Free from what? But of course in a few seconds the feeling went away. Everybody knows what freedom means.

Also I started thinking about *forever*. I'm scared of forever. Forever anything. I think it would bother me if I was told I would *never* be sick, healthy *forever*. But then it occurred to me that forever need never be endured, only one day and another and today. And that doesn't take much time. Anyone who's been both nine and nineteen should have a pretty good idea how fast ten years can go.

Then I heard the radio again, an ad. "GM—Mark of Excellence." I started laughing, thinking of an emendation: "GM—mark of bullshit." It struck me as funny.

At three o'clock I have an appointment to interview the Programming Director of WABC radio, a station perfectly exemplary of the amplitude modulator pop facet of contemporary American culcha.

I am of the opinion that the United States is engaged in a controversial war in Southeast Asia, and that the country has other problems, too. I think people ought at least to think about these things, but I've noticed that the radio medium is a tremendous airy goofball, which anesthetizes everyone who listens. I'm curious about the motivation of the people whose 50,000-watt pump pours such crap into the already polluted air.

The sounds of Summerpower radio wafted over the sidewalk as I approached the ABC building. Fighting to maintain my alertness, I noted that the plants in the lobby were real. Obviously the seat of empire, here. It was one of these places where you know what you're up against as soon as you see the computer-dispatched elevators.

Gold shirts, purple shirts, double-breasted jackets with necktie/handkerchief sets scurried by me.

"Hi, lover."

"Hello, baby."

It seemed the employees were happy. Buckle shoes. Short hair with long sideburns. The entertainment industry on parade.

After I waited half an hour in his corridor (his secretary had ABC playing over a speaker on her desk. Did she have to?), Mr. Sklar invited me in.

Perhaps he thought I'd come with the intention of seizing the station, but for one reason or another he was very edgy and defensive.

I asked him whether he thought his station exerted some kind of influence on its listeners.

"They exert an influence on us and we exert one back," he said, obviously well acquainted with Newtonian physics.

How many teen-agers participate in this interaction? (I feel that radio has a lot to do with the formation of the teen-age mind, such as it is.)

Referring to charts, he told me that in any average quarter hour in an average school-night evening, 125,500 teens (which means aged twelve to seventeen in the radio biz) are listening to WABC, or at least have it on within earshot.

How many teens tune in during a week?

This was a question of "cumes" for which Mr. Sklar turned to his "cume" chart. "Cumes" are figures on the total cumulative number of different individuals who hear the station in a week. The latest "cume" was 1,613,000. These kids are so tuned in that at the mention of a contest they will cough up as many as 150,000 to 200,000 postcards in one week. The Principal of the Year election elicited 25,000,000 individually signed index cards.

I wanted to know why you never hear any peace songs on AM stations—no Ochs, no Collins, no Fish. Peace is a tremendous force in current music, though you never hear about it on the radio.

Mr. Sklar explained that AM stations are programmed according to sales of 45's and those songs are all on albums. FM is programmed by album sales.

Why, I asked, is AM programming determined by 45 sales.

"I thought I explained," said Mr. Sklar, "but I'll go through it once again."

He told me that 45's determine AM, albums FM.

"Hey Sklar," I thought, "where'd you get your name—a sci. fi. novel? Pretty up tight, aren't you, Sklar? Don't mess with the press, Sklar."

I asked him if they censor anything.

"When you buy a book or a ticket," he said, "you're making a choice. When you turn on the radio, you don't know what you're going to hear. Something that might offend people tuning in, not expecting to hear this sort of thing—this might be held."

Just then a young exec underling strode in and asked if it was worth it to ask the D.J.s to call attention to "the psychedelic WABC poster in today's *Daily Column*."

Mr. Sklar wasn't sure it was psychedelic. I was sure it wasn't.

"Well," the exec conceded, "it's sort of a combination of psychedelic and surrealistic."

He was dispatched to chase some money, and I asked why WABC couldn't play a few sounds that weren't popular but perhaps should be, and maybe broaden tastes.

"Because then nobody will listen and we're going for listeners."

I asked Mr. Sklar why they don't play "Sky Pilot" on his station. He said because not enough people seem to be buying it. I think we both knew why people weren't buying it.

I finally told him that I thought people could listen to ABC and never glean that there are problems or challenges in the world more serious than acne or hot, tired feet.

He said "Oh no, there are two newscasts per hour in great detail."

I conceded the two newscasts but expressed a little skepticism about the great detail. ("Canada is still sinking and the Russians have bombed Detroit, now back to the Show.")

He said Well, they "employ specialists to extract the essence of the news. This is a fast-paced world and people want to be given the facts quickly."

I guess he's right. I guess everybody's in a hurry to hear the Cowsills "sing" about their groovy family vacation spot in the Catskills.

Mr. Sklar concluded. "I'm somewhat concerned," he said, sounding very concerned, "about the way some people form generalizations about these areas of frivolity that don't exist. I mean, don't you think people need constructive outlets for healthy recreation, something to dance to?"

"I," I said, "am for that."

Leaving, I picked up some literature on what WABC, as the nation's largest station, can do for advertisers.

The first thing we people should realize about ourselves is that in the WABC primary market area, we represent, in fact we *are*, a "Consumer spendable income" of $78,024,892,000, a figure usually referred to as simply "more than $78 billion," which gives you an idea of what $24,892,000 is worth these days.

Everybody from Cornhusker's Lotion to Chanel No. 5, from Cope and Compoz and the Virginia Department of Conservation to Moral Rearmament and Dr. Golden's Contact Lenses bought their way to our ears via ABC in 1967 .

The man between the advertisers and our wallets is the D.J.

A good D.J. is friendly, congenial and amusing, the sort of person you trust, the sort of person who can get you to spend lots of money you can't afford for things you don't need.

WABC has some of the best.

Dan Ingram, according to a publicity folder, "is solid gold . . . a man able to hammer out the hard sell one minute . . . intone a public service spot the next."

Bob Lewis' (Bob-a-Loo) "many personal appearances for such causes as 'Toys for Tots' sponsored by the Marine Corps, high school hops for civic organizations and stage appearances for fund-raising drives have given him an especially good image in the New York Area. One that will work well for any advertiser."

Chuck Leonard: "His ingenuity with a commercial is becoming legend."

Another booklet was called "The Dynamics of Power," but can you stand any more? They've obviously got it.

Wednesday, July 17: I was reading the Manhattan phone book this morning. Sometimes I read the phone book when I get tired of listening to the correct time tape going through its ticks and tones routine. Reading the directory is more interesting, but listening to the recording is easier. They're both pretty good diversions.

Anyway, on page 1200 there is an ad for the New York Karate Academy. "Kung-fu, Karate, Ju-jitsu, Judo, Boxing, a must for city living."

I'm living in the city. I don't know karate. It remains to be seen if it's really "a must."

A girl I knew used to assure her mother that I'd be all right walking through the city at night because I was a crew jock. I don't know what good that was supposed to do me. Maybe I was supposed to hit muggers over the head with an oar or row away from them.

This afternoon I fled the city for home to try to get some work done on the Book. Very much a *déjà vu* scene, as I was in the same car and again had insufficient cash reserves. Fifty miles from home I calculated that I had to buy fifty cents worth of gas in order to make it. Counting my change, I had precisely fifty cents, not counting the gray penny. Counting my change, I dropped a quarter on the car floor and never saw it again. If they want to get you, you're going to get got. No use fighting it.

I told the gas man my story and he gave me fifty cents worth. Not everyone from Samaria is bad.

Thursday, July 18: Coming into my home I saw a red ant and a black ant struggling on the walk. I thought I might arbitrate the issue by stepping on both of them. That would be an object lesson for them in the uselessness of fighting, but then, it wouldn't do them any good because they'd both be dead. My front walk is the constant theatre of such meaningless little wars. It's a lot like the world, huh?

In the evening I went to Logan Airport to see Short off on his flight to Paris. I went to the observation deck and watched in amazement as people waved and shouted good-bye to various screams and flashes in the sky. I thought that was a pretty good example of twentieth-century depersonalization, but I found a much better one when I tried to return to my car in the airport garage. I found it in thirty-five minutes flat.

Friday, July 19: Reading over the Book I fear I'm giving the impression that I'm hanging loose and bemused and don't overly care about anything. Well, how's this:

Leave me and my friends alone, bastards. Get somebody else to fight your fucking wars. You're up against something here because we're young and won't bend and we're against you. Think twice before you build your next huge mother-fucking turnpike and try to throw people out of their homes because we won't let you. Think twice before you pour your stinking bloody money into more weapons because people are hungry and we won't let you. We need good schools and houses for people to live in and it could be done and we're going to make this country do it. We've had it up to here with you and you don't have much time left, man. We don't even know who you are but we're going to find out. You're playing with fire and fire burns, baby. I mean this. I mean it well. Hear me: you're going to get human or your stinking bodies are going up against the wall. I don't get mad easily but I'm mad now and I'm going to stay mad until things change. You change them, or we change them. I don't care. But the choice isn't going to be yours much longer.

Sorry. I'm not apologizing; I mean I'm sorry that that's the way things are. Anger and hatred is a place I go to sometimes. You're making me live there.

Saturday, July 20: I returned to the City and went with Laura to a Phil Ochs concert in the park.

After listening to Phil Ochs I'm ready not only to burn City Hall, but to charge out and stuff envelopes or distribute leaflets or even sit at a meeting.

During "Rhythms of Revolution," everybody, all the people, looked pensive and feeling rose up and moved from person to person. I was thinking about the letter Laura had suggested I write.

Dear Draft Board,

There must be some mistake here. You can't tell me what to do. I didn't vote for you or select or approve you. Please take my name off your mailing list and stop bothering me.

I was thinking how Mary Smith would react to that one. All my draft stuff is signed "Mary Smith," I swear to God. I don't know whom they think they're kidding.

The park is walled in by skyscrapers. Laura turned to me and said "The buildings are the Biggees you're always talking about. They're watching us. They'll allow you to make as much noise as you want as long as you don't get as tall as they are."

Jim and Jean sang some song about people, and it hit me, really hit me, that we're all people. That makes us really close. I mean there are rocks and lions and lot's of things to be. But we're all people. We're all together in this thing, so we could feel very close to each other about it and say all right, we're all kind of weak and bad but we're going to do the best we can and try to muddle through everything together because there's nowhere to go and there's nothing else to be. That way everyone could be fairly happy because no one would hate anybody. But man, talk about incredibly unrealistic utopian impossibilities!

Sunday, July 21: I was talking with some friends, and one mentioned that a Marine in Vietnam who had been convicted of shooting an old woman had gotten a three-year sentence, while guys who refuse the draft get up to five years. He thought that said something about the values of America.

That does say something about the values of America, but I don't think the Marine should have been punished more. After all, he was trained to expect congratulatory ribbons and stars for killing.

He pleaded temporary insanity, which I think is a true description of how his mind was. Anyone in the Marines is temporarily insane for the three years he's in, maybe for the rest of his life.

"The Marines Make Men" say the recruiting posters. It's true, but incomplete. The Marines make men mad, make them into something they weren't before.

In the Marines you have to wind your belt tightly enough so that the inspecting officer can't see through the hole in the center of the coil. All right. In the Marines you have to wipe out your soap dish so that there is no moisture in the bottom. Fine. But they don't just tell you to do these things, they somehow make you care. Can you imagine listening to some insecure inferiority-complexed officer scream at you about a wet soap dish and you saying "Yes sir" without laughing?

But other things aren't so funny.

From the Parris Island (USMC) yearbook:

MY RIFLE: This is my RIFLE. There are many like it but this one is mine. My rifle is my best friend. It is my life. I must master it as I master my life.

My rifle, without me is useless, without my rifle I am useless.

I must fire my rifle true. I must shoot straighter than my enemy who is trying to kill me. I must shoot him before he shoots me. I will. . . .

My rifle and myself know that what counts in this war is not the rounds we fire, the noise of our burst, nor the smoke we make. We know that it is the hits that count. We will hit. . . .

My rifle is human, even as I, because it is my life. Thus, I will learn it as a brother. I will learn its weakness, its strength, its parts, its accessories, its sights, and its barrel. I will keep my rifle clean and ready, even as I am clean and ready. We will become part of each other.

We will. . . .

Before God I swear this creed. My rifle and myself are the defenders of my country. We are the masters of our enemy. We are the saviours of my life.

So be it, until victory is America's and there is no enemy but Peace!

"Before God!" If Jesus heard that he would puke.

Monday, July 22: I called Bill, who works at Philip Morris. The switchboard operator answered "Call for Philip Morris." "That's very clever," I said. She said "Excuse me?" because she doesn't expect to have anybody ever say anything to her.

I had given Bill a list of words: War, peace, youth, age, because, love, hate, God, life, death, stop, continue, true, false, beautiful, was, will be, is, is, is; and he was going to have a computer put them together in a few thousand combinations, to see if we could get a revelation that way.

But the computer had better things to do, which it certainly should at seventy-five dollars an hour. (That's half again as much as the President makes.)

Received a letter written on the Europe-plane by Short. (*Short* is a person's name. Short is a person.)

I look below me—the Atlantic Ocean. It might as well be the floor. Tiled, dirty, familiar, nothing much. Sunrise three hours after it set was quite a show. However, in general . . . nothing. Atlantic Ocean nothing. Airplane nothing. Even flight movie nothing. Orly nothing. Gendarmes nothing. Jet's earphones into seven different channels of music nothing. Croissants nothing. Vino nothing. Meal after meal of nothing. Cliffies nothing. Hippies nothing. Lady from Kansas sitting next to the Cliffie taking pictures with a Brownie four-flash cube nothing.

In this day (and in this age) there is a certain element of adventure lacking in travel and everything.

Tuesday, July 23: Another hard day at the metaphysical office.

In the morning I walked by a fruit store and there was a man there, and he said to the grocer, "I'd like a dozen lemon-limes," and then the grocer said to him, "Look mister, I can give you

lemons or limes, but there's no such thing as a lemon-lime."
Then the man took a can of shaving cream from a bag and
lathered up the grocer's face, saying "Oh yeah? What do you
call this? Smell it."

For some reason they couldn't satisfy themselves that they
were doing this quite right, so they kept doing it over and over,
for four hours, the 98° weather not withstanding.

I would have considered them crazy and their entire endeavor
a gross waste of time, but for the presence of two cameras, a
microphone, four reflectors, three lights, a make-up artist, a
director, and a full complement of technical assistants, assorted
wretched underlings, and an admiring crowd.

In the evening, Laura, a girl friend of hers and I went to picket
Humper downtown. Laura knows most of the people in New
York City. Whenever we're in public I'm known as the guy with
Laura.

Old Tri-H (I saw a sign "Hypocrite Honkie Humphrey") was
addressing some Biggees at the Waldorf. Another sign pretty
well expressed the theme of the rally: "Keep America Hump-
free." Now I know, I know, old Hubie was quite the civil-rights
trailblazer and all. He's ten years ahead of his time. Unfortunately, his time was 1948. I have lots of rational political dis-
agreements with the man, but basically, he makes me sick.

The red-helmeted loony who had impuned our virility that
time in Low Library had somehow landed the position of M.C.
at this rally. Introducing Jerry Rubin, he said ". . . we care more
about his [cop-]broken disk than about all the broken bones,
dead or alive, in Robert Kennedy." I was amazed. The police
were appalled. The crowd was absolutely silent. If someone had
cheered I would have either punched him or thrown up on him.

Rubin, non-plused, got up to speak. Waving near him was a
very graphic-artsy, black and red Resistance flag and an American
Revolution '76 flag. Which reminds me. You see, in this city
at least, tons of cars, myriad autos, more and more every day,
with American flag decals on the windows. The squad cars all
have them. And everytime I see one I think, God, there goes

another war freak, another support-our-boys-on-their-way-to-the-grave nut, and I go down inside. I think it's too bad that I should be in a position where I demand that cops remove flags from their cars because cops aren't supposed to be political. It's a real down when you get bad vibrations from your own flag. I don't want orgasmic joy from Old Gory either. I just want it to wave up there and I'll live around down here, content to have it above me. So what I would suggest—and this is the only concrete suggestion in the Book—is that all the leftists put flags on their cars too, to de-factionalize the flag, thus depriving the right of one symbol, and also asserting our potential for patriotism, our desire to have a country to be patriotic about.

So there's Rubin, standing behind these flags, and he says, "There is more freedom for a Cuban in one day than most Americans find a lifetime." Rubin has been to Cuba and you and I haven't so let's not pass that off too lightly. He went on to say, "Americans find happiness in other people's unhappiness" and I think that's true.

There were about fifty-sixty McCarthy people picketing Humper on their own, and Rubin said for them that Clean's role is to put us in the system, cool the rebellion in the streets.

It seems to me that, unless rebellion in the streets is an end in itself, and *if* Clean can make the system work, then we shouldn't mind coming in off the streets. The thing is, though, that Clean can't make the system work and if he could, he probably wouldn't unless the rebellion was pushing him. I really don't know.

"Open the jails," he said, "let everybody out, and then put the pigs in jail."

I figure there are, no doubt, many pigs who should be in jail, but not all of them. I hate to hear anybody talk about all of anybody that way. Perhaps if every pig precinct had a different color uniform—pink, pastel blue, white—then people wouldn't lump them all together in the same pen. I'm no cop lover, but saying pigs are all this or pigs are all that reminds me of sentiments like "The only good Indian is a dead Indian," a phrase which produced far too many good Indians.

"America the great power is over," he said, looking very tiny against the skyscrapers.

"The $500-a-plate dinners are over," he said, as he stood outside one. "Come out with your hands up!"

"Up against the wall!" said the crowd.

"Up against the wall!" said the crowd.

"Up against the wall!" said the crowd.

The next speaker was one of your standard strikers from Columbia. (I saw fifteen Columbia kids I knew.) He said there's going to be a Revolution and it's going to be armed. "Ask the Panthers if that ain't true. Dig it babies." He said "ain't" quite frequently and spoke with what I presume he thought was a working man's accent.

"Victory is not around the corner. It's gonna be twenty, thirty, forty, fifty years. It's gonna be our lives. That's what it's gotta be.

"The ballot or the bullet. We know which way we've got to go. There is no democracy in America, not for black people or white people either." But can you institute a free society with guns? Means and ends. Do means shape ends?

Then the black teacher Poynter spoke.

"We're going to do unto others as they've been doing unto us. We're going to even things out a little, start taking care of business in the proper way."

Then the officially permitted rally ended and the leader said we should all go home now, but that there are various ways to go home, which is code for now we're going to march in the streets but we're not going to say so because we don't want to get busted for inciting to riot.

Laura and I marched but her friend went home because she said the whole thing made her sick—all the hatred—which was a very honest thing to say inasmuch as if you want to make it with the activists, hatred is supposed to be all right with you.

Hatred isn't all right with me, but I've seen things such that a little ranting against pigs and Biggees doesn't upset me too much. As a matter of principle, though, I don't think we should return hatred for hatred—people have been doing that too long.

I think we should shower the pigs and the candidates and the Biggees with gifts. We should love them for hating us, we should thank them for caring.

We marched all over the place, screwing up traffic some; and me all the time wondering how this was going to end any wars or feed anybody.

Someone suggested that "It's a Jewish race riot," which you can add to the list of the many unfunny things I've laughed at.

Then the time came as it always does when the cops decide they've had enough and bust people and beat some. I was amazed at how scared I was of the cops. At Columbia I had no fear. Now I had to be brave because all kinds of fright chemicals were coursing around inside me.

Laura and I stood on the corner arm in arm and watched very calmly as the cops grabbed people and twisted their arms behind them and slugged them in the stomach and hit them on the head and also took the flags and tore them and walked on them for some reason. People all around us were getting it but we made as if we were strolling or something. You can fade into the woodwork that way. It wasn't a good demonstration. Normally, Laura marches at the front and grabs onto people who are being clubbed and tries to pull them away from the cops. She gets just upset enough to do that.

We went home. Nothing like a little danger to cement a relationship.

Wednesday, July 24: I was outside this morning and it was pouring water all over the place and I couldn't help remarking my absolute inability to make it stop. I ducked into a restaurant and as I was ordering a cheeseburger, a young woman beside me turned and started talking to me. She must have known you're not supposed to do that, but she didn't seem to care.

She asked me what month I was born. September. She wanted to know what day. I said the twenty-third. "That's Libra," I said, assuming that was what she was thinking about.

"You're a cusp," she said.

"A what?" (Teeth?)

"A cusp. Do you know what that is? It means you were born on the day the sign changes."

"What does that make me?"

"You're both."

She asked me if I went to school. I told her Columbia and she asked me how I felt about the demonstrations. I told her I was in them. She asked me again how I felt about them. I said they were all right. She asked me if I saw one side or two sides. I said I saw two sides. In fact, I said, that's why I can't be too close with the radicals sometimes. I just don't feel as sure of myself as they seem to feel about themselves.

Then she asked me if I thought progress was fast or slow. I said scientific progress is fast, because it builds on itself. The curve goes like this, I said, tracing a hyperbole in the air. Acceleration of history. Social progress is slow. It's practically nonexistent. We're about where we were 10,000 years ago. But you have to try to make it go fast so that it will go slow at all.

Do you think evolution is going on, she asked next. I said sure evolution is always going on. Civilization hasn't stopped evolution. But she meant evolution of minds. Oh, I said, yes. Because today an incomparably greater number of people than ever before don't have to worry about food or clothing or shelter, so they're free to think. Also, a vastly greater number of kids are in college now. What's important is not so much what they learn, but just that they're all together in a community to develop their ideas, instead of being all spread around. So I do expect changes.

She agreed but wanted to know what I thought the year twenty-thirty would be like. I said I'd be dead then.

You don't give yourself much time, she said. About seventy-five years—is that from statistics?

No, I said, it's from what I feel like. I wouldn't want to live too long as a vegetable.

But wouldn't I be curious to see what happens. I said that's irrelevant because no matter how long you live, you're not going to live to the year after that and you can't really see anything, because the vast preponderance of time will transpire after you've died.

Well, what did I think it would be like?

It would be very different from now. Just by 2000, people will be working a six-hour week. Also, they'll shop by dialing computers, and not have to move around, and wear plastic shoes. We're the last generation to share in the human heritage. We have to work and move. We're more close to the people of 100 A.D. than to those of 2030.

The Last of the Mohicans, she said. I thought that was a good way of putting it.

We're the bridge generation, I continued. We're the product of all the past and we'll determine all the future.

Depressing or what?

No, it's exciting. It's a challenge. It's up to us to keep future people human, assuming that's desirable.

Is it?

I don't know. I mean, in *Brave New World* the people were all always happy. They were dehumanized and low but the fact remains they were happy. It was repugnant to the observer, but they couldn't step outside their system to see. They were just happy. That seems all right.

Do people ever step back from their systems and look?

No, I don't think so. Not most of them. If they did, they wouldn't do what they do.

Are you enjoying your life?

Am I enjoying my life? (Nobody had ever asked me that before. I'm not sure what it means.) Yeah, I'd say so. I wasn't last fall. I was completely uninterested in anything. I went around smashing things all the time.

What made you change?

I changed all my courses. The new courses weren't important; it was the changing. I could start all over. Also, it stopped being winter eventually and the days got longer. Now things are kind of exciting. My star seems to have risen, I said, knowing she'd be pleased by the use of the astrological metaphor. But sometimes I wish I didn't have to write the Book (I had told her about the Book), because I don't know anything.

I know, she said, and I believe she did know.

I look up in my head and there's this great emptiness, a void; there's nothing there. I don't know anything.

I know, she said.

And I was reading Erich Fromm, and I thought it was good, but it made me despair of ever knowing anything, because he knows so much. He knows everything.

Erich Fromm, she said, tells how. He describes how. But he doesn't tell why.

I asked her how she happened to start talking to me. Does she always talk to whoever is sitting beside her?

No. She saw something in my eyes. A certain look.

Oh, I said.

You've been chewed up and spit out, she said. A couple of times.

I know that, I said. I've been through some of the big chomping machines.

That's why, she said.

That's why? I asked.

That's why, she explained.

I went home and looked in the mirror at my eyes.

Thursday, July 25: I got up in the morning and went to a session of the Cox Fact-Finding Commission. State Senator Basil Paterson was testifying about his dealings with the blacks holding Hamilton Hall during the siege of Columbia, which I vaguely remember having taken place once upon a time.

He talked about how President Kirk had offered the blacks a deal whereby if they came out they would not be suspended expelled or legally prosecuted. I probably would have been upset about this discrimination—there were no deals with us— if I had known about it at the time, but as someone told me, "The white students weren't about to get the city burned." It seems that there was reason to be concerned that the occupation might have grown into something bigger. The police had told Kirk they wanted everything settled by 6 P.M. the first day. The senator said the black students were very concerned lest they be expelled. (The whites, I'd say, didn't worry about it too much. A white radical can always get into some other school.) He also stressed that there weren't more than two or three community people (Outside Agitators) in Hamilton.

The head of the Joint Committee on Disciplinary Affairs was questioned next. He said his committee had made "a rather categorical demand" that criminal trespass charges be dropped, but the Trustees were adamantly opposed to that. At that point the Committee "had either to resign or find a way to live with it." They didn't resign.

In response to a question the disciplinarian replied that from May 15 to May 28 he could remember "nothing substantive that was done publicly." Cox said that it sounded as though perhaps something had been done privately. But the man adamantly maintained that his committee had accomplished absolutely nothing.

At the second Hamilton bust, Dean Coleman announced that anyone arrested would be automatically suspended. That seemed to Mr. Cox to deprive the Discipline Committee of any function. But the head of it said "No one had given us any direction on how to consider Coleman's statement. We could have ignored it."

"Was that a viable choice?" asked Cox.

"I have no idea," replied the man. The man was smoking more and more.

I hadn't been over to Strike Central, or the Liberation School, or SDS, or the place, or whatever you wish to call it, for eons, so I went over and talked to Dan who hangs on pretty well and can usually tell you what's going on, although not necessarily correctly. He said "The strike newspaper has only come out once. It's really hierarchical. Rudd picked the staff. Rudd's a nice guy but he's such an elitist.

"The Strike Education Committee people were edged out

of the Liberation School organization. It became more and more narrow and elitist. A teacher was told he couldn't teach courses because he didn't have the right line.

"Were you at the march Thursday? [No.] Oh, fantastic! Rudd's up there and he says 'Hell, let's do something. To Harlem!' Four hundred people marched. There was no point to it. Of course not.

"Rudd got up at the rally and started insulting liberals. He said the Students for a Restructured University leaflet wasn't worth wiping his ass with. Of course liberals are the most masochistic people around. So they went into the streets chanting 'Ho, Ho, Ho Chi Minh, Columbia Strike is going to win.' They felt guilty.

"About two hundred blacks joined in, but they weren't the most savory types. When they got back to Columbia they wanted some action. Rudd got scared.

"Blacks in the movement criticized it. You don't go into Harlem telling the blacks what to do unless you're willing to go along with them.

"The whole thing was sort of a carnival. Rudd's so confused when things happen. He came back saying 'Well, maybe we should have smashed some windows.'

"The Labor Committee thought it was mindless activism. The activists thought 'Where's the Labor Committee. They're holding discussions while we're in Harlem.'

"Rudd gets all the publicity. He's very charismatic. It's hard to say how much power he has. Just before we left for the SDS National Convention, J.J. took over the Liberation School. It was a real putsch.

"You get guys up here analyzing the liberal mentality, and they haven't been near one in years.

"Rudd's very bright, but he's very confused. He gets carried away . . . Rudd knows what he's doing. He's a good guy. He has ideas of his own, but he usually lets other people propose ideas and then he goes along with them.

"The main criticism of the action faction is that they have no program. Now *Papert* has a program.

"Rudd's a good guy, but he has too many flaws—rough around the edges. But he'll develop into a good leader some day."

Of course no one ever finishes talking quite that abruptly, but essentially the interpersonal information transfer ended there, and I went out, but not before seeing a letter re: me, on the wall. It was a letter, on Columbia U. stationery, to Allen Burke of TV infame.

Dear Mr. Burke,

Congratulations on your show on Columbia this morning. It was a GREAT show. You said so rightly and so effectively to rebel James Kunan what we—the great majority (faculty and students) at Columbia—want to say to him and his like. Yours is the Voice of Justice, and your show is unique in TV industry because of it.

We faculty members of Columbia who have long been associated with and sentimentally attached to this great University and its Administration have been dealt with unspeakable injustice recently by the power-mad SDS minority groups and their blind and emotional sympathizers. The forces of evil at Columbia have been so strong and their voice so loud that they threaten either to eclipse the good deeds of the Administration through the years, or to drown the voice of righteousness . . . How we depend on you to further the cause of justice in this mad society of injustice and violence, a society of which the moral fabric is almost torn beyond repair.

> With admiration for your courage, a naturalized citizen,
> lover of Columbia and U.S.A.,
> and intense hater of SDS.

Everywhere haters. I got an anonymous letter from the Bronx which started "Mr. Kumen, You and your kind are a disgrace to the human race." It went on to suggest that I drown myself, but only after I submit to beatings by cops and "decent fellows at Columbia." You should see some of the letters Rudd gets.

In the afternoon Laura and I flew to Boston to go to a Clean Rally at Fenway Park.

We got in, but there were people sitting in all the aisles and about 10,000 disgruntling outside the park. A typical American move—Clean sold every seat twice.

It wouldn't have been sufficient to be able to say it was a sellout. Every seat had to be filled. If someone got into an auto accident on the way, there had to be someone to rush in to his seat for him.

It was a press event. The field was crawling with press. We, looking at the tiny figure in a box at second base, were just a back-drop and sound effects machine.

The sound effects machine was comprised of all kinds of middle-class people, very few hair people, no one in uniform, no one who looked like a laborer, and no blacks. Except in the program. The program was loaded with blacks.

In front of me was a hippie with his grandmother. That makes it.

Pete Seeger sang "If I Had a Hammer" and asked the people to sing along, which they did. They were all happy in being together—ending war and having a nice night out. I wasn't happy with them but I was kind of happy.

Clean gave his usual non-speech. He said that Humper "says he doesn't know what my program for peace is. Well they seemed to know what it was in New Hampshire and Wisconsin and Oregon." Everybody cheered. People applaud the most banal nothings. I was wondering what his program for peace was. He didn't say; he just said that we knew.

He kept referring to the war as "unwise."

But he said one thing that I took with me. He said if we are to make mistakes, let our mistakes be on the side of trust, and not mistrust. I figure you'll make more mistakes that way but you'll have a better time doing it and you might get somewhere, perhaps forward.

On the flight back to the city we saw Paul O'Dwyer, Mc-Carthy-supporting incredible upset fiery radical character Democratic Senatorial Nominee from New York.

I congratulated him on the huge turnout in Boston and said "I'm a disaffected young radical, but if anything's going to re-affect me it'll be you and Senator McCarthy."

"I think we can give you a run for your money," he said.

"I hope so." (You see I have no wish to have to be hassled with revolutions. If some good man would take care of everything, I'd be glad to let him handle it.)

"Stay radical," he said, "but don't be disaffected."

Was that great? Was that fine advice? I liked it.

He invited me to come down to his headquarters and, touching Laura, said, "You come too, we could use some charm." (He doesn't lack for charm. Laura went to work there forty hours a week as volunteer coordinator.)

"Who's John Elder?" he asked me, looking at my campaign button.

"I haven't any idea," I answered.

Back home Laura and I were excited or at least vaguely pleased at having rubbed elbows with the mighty. "Let's save these ticket stubs," I said. "They may be very old some day."

Friday, July 26: Up at Columbia I walked into a room where J.J. and Tom Hayden and Lew Cole were talking and they told me I'd have to leave. The concepts of participatory democracy and of the revolutionary vanguard are not easily reconciled.

I called the telephone business office, just to pass the time, and asked why pay phones don't make change for quarters.

The woman said "No, they don't make change. If you put in a quarter, you're not going to get anything back."

"Why?" I asked.

"They're not equipped to."

"How come?"

"Because they don't make them that way."

I thanked her and then called Bill.

I had gotten into a situation regarding the physical defense of my honor, which is another way of saying my pride, which is another way of saying my ego. Yesterday I called Bill, a long-time friend and now spiritual adviser, and he promised he'd have an answer for me today. It was a two-part answer.

Part I. Three things in ascending importance are: 1) thoughts 2) words 3) actions.

Part II. None of these are of any importance whatsoever. That straightened me right out.

I went to the Bureau of Applied Social Research to find out how their social research applied to the strike was coming along. They asked me what I wanted to know and I said I didn't know. Maybe I'd come in again Monday. They gave me a questionnaire to fill out. Also they asked me how I felt about SDS and I said I didn't like them. The Students for a Restructured University (liberals)? I didn't like them either. "As a matter of fact," I said, "everybody's losing favor with me." They said great, I could join the anarchistic free spirits. I said I didn't like anarchistic free spirits. They asked me what I thought of the administration, and I said it was a lot like the Grand Coulee Dam—no intelligence whatsoever.

I called for an appointment with Vice-President Truman, but was told he's on vacation for a month. He's probably in a basement closet in Low Library. I was given an appointment with Dean Herbert Deane.

I had no idea who Herbert Deane was, so I went around asking random people.

"He does something around here" was the first response. They were all like that:

"Isn't there a Dean Deane? He must be the Dean Deane."

"That's a nice name. Who is he?"

"Dean Deane. That's terrific."

You might say that Dean Deane is not exactly in the mainstream of Columbia life. But then, no one is. There is no mainstream of Columbia life. Columbia is a lot of meandering rivulets up which the students struggle, vainly attempting to spawn.

Saturday, July 27: Sorry, no Revolution for me today. Today I'm rather more dead than red. I've got a summer cold, which is broadly acknowledged to be a different animal.

I went to Central Park to soak up some D-rays, and I ran into bumped into came across met without prearrangement a friend of mine from Columbia U. I asked him who Herbert Deane was, or is, for that matter.

"Deane? Deane. Isn't he the one who made the Strawberry Statement?"

"Of course!" I said. "He's the one who made the statement about IDA!"

"And strawberries," my friend said.

Sunday, July 28: I rolled down my sleeves because I was cold, and then I rolled them up because I was warm, and then it occurred to me that I had come upon a new and novel mode of gentle exercise to pass the time. It didn't stay novel very long. I got bored with the whole idea after fifteen circuits.

Everybody's pretty pissed off about the way things are these days, but today I came across something we should all be grateful for. *Water puts out fire.* I threw a cigarette in the toilet, and it went right out. That struck me as very convenient and very fortunate. No one appreciates stuff like that. I mean, suppose it exploded?

Suppose the only thing that would extinguish fire was goat's milk. Or diamonds. That would be really dangerous. Firemen would have to go around picking up all their diamonds after every fire. Or more likely, everything would have burned up a long time ago.

But water is readily available and easily transported and cheap enough to be well within the means of anybody who has to put something out. That's a real break, I think.

In the evening I went up to the U. to check out a strategy

meeting. A kid was giving a report on an SDS convention. He said that J. Edgar Hoover had said that we were as big a threat as the Communist Party. This evoked peals of laughter, as we consider the C.P. to be a stodgy old group who are no threat at all compared to us.

The Hoov reported to Congress that there was, at this convention, a workshop on sabotage. There was, but the only people there were the guy who called it plus the sixteen other FBI agents and an SDS guy who was sent to keep an eye on them.

There was some chagrin expressed at the convention that Columbia SDS had on its own piddling initiative called the First International Students' Conference, to be held at C.U. in the fall.

"New York is like looked on as a real insane place," the kid said. "People are always surprised if they like someone from New York.

"Also at the convention, men from Business International Roundtables—the meetings sponsored by *Business International* for their client groups and heads of government—tried to buy up a few radicals. These men are the world's leading industrialists and they convene to decide how our lives are going to go. These are the guys who wrote the Alliance for Progress. They're the left wing of the ruling class.

"They agreed with us on black control and student control. They were for kicking out Kirk. Only thing they disagreed with us on was imperialism. They figure we've got the technology the world needs, and we ought to have some control over where it goes and for what.

"They want McCarthy in. They see fascism as the threat, see it coming from Wallace. The only way McCarthy could win is if the crazies and young radicals act up and make Gene look more reasonable. They offered to finance our demonstrations in Chicago.

"We were also offered Esso (Rockefeller) money. They want us to make a lot of radical commotion so they can look more in the center as they move to the left."

I found out at this meeting that *Life* is doing a five-part article on SDS in the fall. The article is supposed to be favorable, and they want our cooperation. This information was received with passionate, almost moral, disapproval: Such coverage would "relegate us to the route of the hippies. Next thing they'd have Mark Rudd sweatshirts. After that they have an issue on the radical right. So it turns out you get an issue every five weeks on a different bunch of nuts."

It was obvious to everyone that what *Life* is trying to do is co-opt us. And I always thought they were trying to sell magazines.

Monday, July 29: Considerably before I awakened, at 10 A.M., I went to see Dean Deane. He kept me waiting a decent amount of time, then invited me in.

The first thing I said was that he shouldn't worry about me misquoting him, because I wouldn't quote him at all. I was lying. I had every intention of quoting him. I had no intention of doing anything but quote him.

He said people come in all the time who want to talk about changing the University, but don't even know how it is run now. "If one more person asks me what the University Council is, I'll yell," he said. That made me afraid to ask him.

I asked him what the strikers have gained.

"They gained a great deal of attention. It's one major reason groups undertake this type of action. Also there was a certain radicalization on campus. Their support increased."

What did they lose?

"Many people became aware of them and reacted negatively . . . terrifying shift to Wallace. (I don't say SDS caused this.) . . . intense feeling reflected in the mail we get in an average day . . . I don't see Lenin's objective conditions for revolution . . . afraid you scare middle-class labor."

I said I hadn't heard any word about the University getting out of IDA.

"IDA was a symbolic issue. The University never had a research contract with IDA, and the University is no longer a member of IDA. Cold-bloodedly, I think there are far more important ties in the fifty-sixty million dollar per year Government-University contracts."

The dependence of science on the government worries Dean Deane.

"But we're far less dependent than many universities," he pointed out. "M.I.T., for example, couldn't survive six months without government money. Here, tenure salaries don't come from government money."

I asked him if the gym was dead. Everybody tells me it is.

"For good or evil," he said, "for better or worse, it's finished." He emphasized the *evil* and the *worse* and looked sort of sad and distant.

"There is no possibility of resumption. The only possibility is a gym under different auspices. . . . A black leader asked us 'Who is going to build the gym for the kids?' After all the rhetoric's gone, what are the kids going to have?

"The Trustees were very reluctant to go into the park to begin with. Politicians urged them in, to avoid relocation problems."

It's too bad this last statement didn't mention fruit or it could have become immortal too. I'm not saying it isn't true. I don't know if it's true. I don't even know if I was really talking to Dean Deane. For all I know, there is no Dean Deane. But the man delivered the lines without batting an eyelash, without acknowledging or caring that I had heard and read and seen evidence to the contrary and would have great difficulty and little inclination to believe him. That is the special flare all Biggees have—they can walk right through a wall if they didn't build it.

I shook that one off and asked him if he subscribed to the opinion that the whole action had been coolly plotted well in advance at some smoke-filled SDS meeting. He didn't.

"SDS is not a very hierarchically organized institution. It's a very mixed bag. There was a lot of ad-hoc-ing going on. We're all getting paranoid enough."

Is the administration anticipating trouble in the fall?

"I think one has to. I assume that the thirty or forty will pursue their course."

("The thirty or forty" is the administration name for the campus' five hundred most militant students.)

"The question is how the thousands of sympathetic will act. I'm sure if we have a pattern of disruption of University life, many faculty are going to quietly leave. They simply won't live in this kind of atmosphere."

But wouldn't they run into the same thing at other schools?

"If a school doesn't have these problems, it's dead. But some faculty have deep emotional attachments to this idiot place" (which makes it more of a strain for them when things go wrong).

"If you could name a university where students aren't concerned with Vietnam and the cities," he continued, "I'd be scared to death of the place."

He talked of the bitter frustration and sense of impotence he felt students feel.

"Because they're young they feel everything more sharply, more deeply. One has to find a substitute target for the institutions that won't move. A university is permissive and very fragile; very easy to bring to a halt.

"Three times in twenty years I've had to tell a student to stop talking or please leave. Then suppose he said no, or up against the wall? Then what do I do?"

He was saying, then, that the administration really wasn't equipped to deal with disorder?

"You," he said, "and anyone else around here would have been very horrified if we had been ready."

What mistakes, would he say, did the administration make?

"It would take two hours to go over them. It probably would have been better to be more active earlier.

"The Ad Hoc faculty group was not very helpful, in fact it

confused things . . . twenty-five amateur negotiators. The students didn't know what was being said and who had the authority to say it.

"A young faculty member said 'First we'll settle this, then the war.' That's a vice of the profession—academics are good with words. But they're not usually in a position where their words have any consequence. We write, we talk, we criticize. Academics don't usually make very good politicians."

He was pretty skeptical about student-faculty power.

"Some great proponents of faculty power will say 'You don't expect me to be here in the summer, do you?' And students—how much time and energy can they spend on university problems and remain a student? They could spend sixty to seventy hours a week on administration. The faculty hasn't wanted to wield power. They've wanted to do their thing."

I hadn't realized that youth talk had filtered up this high.

"If anybody, student or faculty, wants to come in here and worry about the five and a half million dollar deficit we've been operating under, God love them. I'd love to share it."

With this the interview collapsed beneath the weight of its own irrelevance, and we just rapped for a while. He asked me, assuring me that he was not looking for "intelligence," what I thought would happen in the fall, and I said, "Oh, I don't know, desire for a return to normalcy versus better organization, competing factors, the usual." Then we talked about the lack of adventure and of physical challenge in contemporary life and he figured this might have something to do with kids jumping around in the streets these days.

He offered to help me get interviews with others and I thanked him for his time.

God, what am I going to do? I *liked* Dean Deane.

I had lunch with a kid who works in the Engineering Dean's office.

"Hear anything?" I asked.

"Yeah. There are going to be 400 tactical police on twenty-four-hour standby in the fall. I hear the phrase 'nip in the bud' used quite frequently. What you should do," he suggested, "is move to another college and incite a revolution, then write about that."

I agreed. I'd have my own salaried group. A couple of radicals, some provocateurs, a few brutal cops. . . .

I went back to the sociologists to see what kind of a profile they've got on me and my kind. They'd had some difficulty getting cooperation from the radical leaders. "They think any clarity that's shed on the situation will be to their disadvantage. We'd approach them and they'd say 'How come you're doing a survey? Why aren't you out on the barricades?' "

They were undaunted, however, and had collected 232 replies, which is impressive. Have you ever tried to get 232 people to do anything? And this was a very long questionnaire.

One of the first questions on it asked about oppression in the U.S. Sixty-three percent of the strikers said they'd had first-hand experience of it, and thirty-two percent were intellectually aware of it.

"Do you think Columbia is a good place to go to school?" was another question I expressed interest in.

"We'll do some comparative analysis," said Ray the sociologist. "Taking everything into account, well over three-quarters, or three-quarters, said yes. And three-quarters said they would choose Columbia again. Strikers don't dislike Columbia any more than non-strikers."

It seems that radicals are better students than non-radicals. Mothers support their children's politics much more than fathers do. Not draft status, but opinions on the war, affect who protests. This Ray called the contextual effect, and he said it was good. Only five percent of students and faculty support either Humper or The Dick for President. And the open-ended question (to which you write an answer rather than blacken a box) show that "the movement isn't nihilistic but very positive, very clear. The leaders just harangue you and you can't make much of it, but the rank and file's comments are articulate and convincing. People have well-defined goals and programs and ideas." That's what Ray told me.

Then he told me that when the Book appears, "They'll be after you. You're an ideologue."

"What's an ideologue?" I asked, wanting to know what I was.

"Someone who makes ideologies," he said, with undisguised admiration for that particular line of work.

"And what's worse, you're in this anarchistic thing, so when they try to get you they won't know where to stamp." He stamped the floor uncertainly in a few different places.

"Were you at the Harlem march?" he asked me. "It was a lot of fun."

I wasn't there, but I thought it would be fun to hear a description to compare to Dan's.

"Absolutely no point whatsoever. It was great. These reporters were walking around saying (he talked into his fist) 'Now they're planning this and now they're planning that.' I said to one, 'Look, nobody's planning anything. It's completely anarchistic. Everybody does whatever he pleases.' He didn't believe me. I told him to go to the front of the crowd and lead us wherever he wanted. At that point we were marching around Low Library for the second or third time."

Ray thought the whole Columbia thing would make a great play, a fantastic play, in fact beyond doubt the best play ever written. He related to me the last scene (taken from life) of Act I—The Ad Hoc Faculty Sandwich Decision.

It is very late at night, virtually early in the morning. The Ad Hoc faculty group has been meeting through the night. They are in their second hour of debate on *what to do about the sandwiches*.

The jocks have surrounded Low Library. Outside the jocks stand angry pukes who want to get food to the protesters inside. White-armbanded Ad Hoc fac. stand tensely between the jocks and the building, unsure what to do, waiting for The Sandwich Decision.

Back at the meeting, rapprochement has been reached between dissident factions. Votes have been taken. The chairman reads the committee's decision:

If a sandwich-carrier tries to cross the hedge, he may be stopped by the jocks.

But, if he should reach the ledge, he may no longer be stopped by the jocks.

THE HEDGE IS THE JOCKS', THE LEDGE IS THE PUKES'.

Curtain
End Act I

Predictably, I left.

Outside I saw two guys standing beside a meter maid, booing and hissing her as she wrote a ticket. She didn't seem moved.

"Rolls right off her back," I said.

"Yeah," replied one, "but she'll sleep on it tonight."

Thence I visited a friend.

"My mother said," he complained, "that as much as I might like it to, the world doesn't turn on English literature and philosophy. She said I ought to go out and learn something for a change. She said I ought to take *economics*."

"I think she's right," I said.

"So do I," he said.

Walked past the bookstore, and in the window were a number of books with a drawing of a very old and wise man, just his face, on the cover. "Scientology is here to rescue you," advised a sign.

I was interested, but not to the point of going in. I remembered the subway posters, "Step into the exciting world of the totally free. Call 565-3878. Scientology works."

I went home. My phone sat smugly (insofar as an inanimate object can be smug) on the floor. All right, I said, I'll call.

The phone rang. I heard the self-satisfied damn-the-torpedoes-full-speed-ahead hello of a tape recorder. "Have you a problem you can do without?" That was it. NO. I have a problem I *can't* do without. Any -ology that's that inane isn't going to get into my life, not this boy.

The old woman from down the hall asked me what I'm going to call the Book.

I said maybe "Up Against the Wall."

She looked displeased. "Sounds too much like *The Wailing Wall*. People will dig into it. *The Wailing Wall* came out twenty years ago."

I told her I'd give it some thought.

Tuesday, July 30: I passed a store called "Hard-to-Get Records." I wonder if they have easy-to-get records. If they don't that makes them hard to get, in which case they should have them.

I wandered up to Columbia and drifted into a Strike Steering Committee meeting.

Mark Rudd, who is among other things Chairman of the Sanitation Committee, was talking.

"The politics has been shitty. The organization has been shitty. The Strike School up to now has been a marshmallow."

With that I went to the *Spectator* offices to satisfy myself that the Strawberry Statement did, in reality, so to speak, exist.

On March 21, 1967, Ralph Halford, Dean of Graduate Faculties, denied any connection between the University and the Institute for Defense Analysis.

Ten days later, the Columbia *Spectator* revealed that Columbia was affiliated, that several faculty members were engaged in secret research, and that there was a secret research facility in Pupin Hall (a building which already bears the distinction of having been the birthplace of the atom bomb).

The article quoted Norman L. Christeller, vice-president and general manager of IDA: "We consider Columbia to be one of the three or four primary sponsors of the IDA. President Kirk has always been an active member of our board."

That was the golden spike. That was the red button. That was the celestial firing cap, the interstellar trigger mechanism, the electromagnetic ignition key, the super sky switch which blended all the currents which had for so long been wending their way together. From the germination of the first strawberry to the purchase of Manhattan, the birth of Grayson Kirk's maternal great-grandfather to Mark Rudd's application essay on extracurricular activities, the first billy club turning on the lathe, the racial bifurcation of American society—all the myriad particles of history and evolution streaming down the reality cables of the universe. With this revelation all was finally in readiness, and on April 25, 1967, the Strawberry Statement sprang from the lips of Dean Deane, to absolutely no effect whatever.

"A university is definitely not a democratic institution," Professor Deane began. "When decisions begin to be made democratically around here, I will not be here any longer."

Commenting on the importance of student opinion to the administration, Professor Deane declared, "Whether students vote 'yes' or 'no' on an issue is like telling me they like strawberries."

I like strawberries.

But July 30 didn't stop with the reading of the Strawberry Statement, any more than April 24, 1967, stopped with the pronouncement of it.

I went back to my unfit-for-human-habitation tenement pad and was visited by Laura and together we called a friend of hers to find out what your typical bopper thinks of Mark Rudd.

I spoke to her first. She said she thought he was a remarkable person. I asked her why, seeing as how she had never met him. She said because of what he's done. I asked her just what he had done, but I didn't press that question, because she had no idea and was embarrassed about it.

"Are you in the movement?" I asked, to change the subject.

"What movement?" she answered.

"The Movement," I urged.

"Not too much," she admitted.

"Are you a liberal?" I asked, seeing if she could handle a curve ball, as it were, to use a baseball metaphor.

"Oh definitely," she asserted, for a called third strike.

Speaking to Laura, she expressed an intense desire to meet Rudd and got very excited when led to believe she might do so, this based on her conviction that "He's cute."

Shortly afterwards, July 30 kind of ended.

You got that? Well, get this—

Wednesday, July 31: I awoke with recollections of a dream in which I kept receiving huge packages with four-by-five foot books in them. I thought the gigantic books were an artful device to express my book anxiety. The dream was well-composed and imaginative. Good job, subconscious mind.

I went downtown to Bryant Park, 5th Avenue and 42nd Street, to meet a friend for lunch. I never found him, so to pass the time and make the trip down worth it, I went around asking people if they knew who Mark Rudd was.

The first girl I asked had never heard of him. I explained that he was the leader of the thing up at Columbia. "What thing?" she wanted to know. "You know," I said, "the Columbia action." She didn't know. She had never heard of the Columbia action. She said she was from California, which seemed a poor excuse to me.

I asked three office girls, and they had never heard of him. I asked a young exec; he didn't have the slightest idea who he was. I was afraid to ask an old exec.

I asked a shoeshine boy. He didn't know. A nun didn't know. A Japanese tourist with a Japanese camera didn't speak English, but he shook his head that he didn't know.

I asked seven young blacks in iridescent green pants. One of them did know who Rudd was, and he was joined by the other six in supporting him all the way.

I asked a park worker. He said he didn't know. I told him. Rudd was a Columbia leader. "I don't think much of Columbia, let's put it that way." I thought that was a good way to put it because he didn't say he didn't like Columbia radicals, or that he didn't like the demonstrations, he just said he didn't like the whole scene, which is compatible with most views.

A little old man with a lot of white hair did know who Rudd was, but he was very emphatic about having no opinion about him or anything else.

A black mailman also knew who Rudd was. But he wouldn't want to give an opinion. "I didn't give it much direct attention," he said, "but I think the students must have had a reason for doing what they did." I thanked him very much for that.

Then I went to Columbia to talk to a kid on Trustee Temple's committee. It became evident, once it was pointed out to me, that there was this thing called the Temple Committee. I had once been aware of the Temple Committee, but how much time do I have to think about things? I have a finite amount of time to think about things and I apparently hadn't been able to work in the Temple Committee. But then someone mentioned it, and now, now it all comes back to me.

The Trustees decided that they wanted to take the view of students into consideration when they planned restructuring of the University, so they asked that students elect representatives to a committee, the Temple Committee. The election-holders held an election, but scarcely anybody came. Everybody figured that the Trustees just wanted to be able to say they'd talked to students, then do precisely whatever they wanted to do. The Trustees wanted to use the students to legitimatize whatever they finally did or did not do. I remember that's what I thought. And only 411 of 2700 students in the college voted.

But the Temple Committee exists so I went to talk to a kid on it, to ask him how he was and how it was and things generally. I arrived at Columbia to find a young man preaching at the gate, which is not unusual, with a microphone and amplifier, which is. He had a scholarly accent and also a sign reading

"Christ for Columbia, Columbia for Christ." He was staring and gesticulating at the crowd, but there was no crowd. People walked right by. That didn't seem to bother him, although it may well have, in fact.

I left. I had to go, really. I was in a hurry.

I hurried to 401 Low Library, a room marked "Radio and Television," to see this kid Bercaw.

I saw a guy who I knew had to be Bercaw, and told him I'd like to speak to Mike Bercaw.

"Try Roy," he said.

I ventured "Roy." That was it all right.

"How often are you meeting with the Trustees?" I asked Roy, realizing as I spoke the words that the frequency of his meetings with the Trustees meant little, in fact absolutely nothing, to me. I noticed that he had a paid secretary and several phones, none of which worked.

He was telling me about the last meeting. ". . . it was a big zoo. It was like a circus," he was saying.

One of the Committee's problems, he felt, was the Columbia College kids on it. "Most of the people in the College are very bright, but they're also very young. [He's twenty-five.] They don't know how little things make things work. Rudd, for instance, knows much better."

He sent for some cookies and iced tea.

"They put our picture in *The New York Times*, playing it up big that they're meeting with students, when they're really not doing anything. Big farce. All they ever say is 'Let's hear some workable proposals.'"

He wasn't going to come up with proposals without some info from the Trustees, and not then until after a decent amount of time transpired. Workable proposals don't grow on trees, to use an arboricultural figure. That does it. I can't write.

I'm trying to quit smoking. Ever try to quit smoking? Ever wish you hadn't started to kill yourself so you wouldn't be having to stop?

Man, you should see my handwriting right now. I know. I

know. Some people quit after twenty years. I don't have such a challenge. I don't know where smoking is at.

Maybe. Maybe not. Maybe if I hadn't been told about nic fits I'd never have any. Maybe I wouldn't feel my lungs having a cat and dog fight, mauling each other, clawing and scratching up the inside of my chest which is what's happening right now.

Oh man. Oh you goddamn Southern agrarian economic interests. You mother-fucking tobacco lobby. Government! GOVERNMENT! I want you to outlaw tobacco advertising.

What?????

That's right. Free speech, okay, but you can't yell fire in a crowded tobacco warehouse without giving cancer to everybody around.

I know. I know. The livelihood of several whole states depends on killing people slowly. Maybe the whole country. In fact I heard the shit-eating department of something agriculture or something has films to teach backward Polynesian and other exotic pot-ope-what-have-you smokers how sexy it is to smoke grettes so we can expand the market which, to borrow a term from another area of government endeavor, might be called a free kill zone.

Well I'll tell you once more, I don't want to see one more cigarette ad, not one. Not in the papers or the mags or on the giant Ladybird-defying ugly billboards. God especially I'll throw a rock through it if I see one more goddamn one on the T.V. Salem especially. God obscenity. Yes Obscen-I-T-Y, plastic (a cliché but describing a cliché) sterile straight people who finally got out of the city to the country and they're there in the oxygen-giving green earth mother virginal yet mother forests SMOKING. Can you hack it? Can you hack it? They're in the country, in the spring in fact, by flowered fields and they're smoking! Well each to his own working out of his death wish, I guess, but don't show that shit to me. I'm serving notice. I'll have no more of it. Too many kids starting all around, you'll see them chained to a pack, being enjoyed by a cigarette, looking silly as a matter of fact if you stop to look but that's neither here nor there, they're

dying, killing themselves, but no, they're being murdered. Homo-
cide! Don't deny it fella. I don't want to hear it. I know, people
don't *have* to smoke. They don't have to be yellow either, I
suppose, which I grant you, all right, I admit, is a wild irrelevant
comparison but only on the surface, man. If you stop to think
you'll see it's all one; it's all not caring about killing people for
a little mon ($). You've got me to answer to now. The war, the
war is a big hassle to stop, I hate it, I'll continue to give those I
can reach a hard time about it, but cancerettes, man, that is to be
ended. I've decided to give you one month to castrate (de-sex.
No one ever got laid for his grette, no one ever made out better
at even one end; how Winston made it long is of no concern
to copulation-seekers. Silva-thins never got anybody in bed).
Where was I, oh yes. Okay. That's clear, right? One month
from publication of this book cigarette advertising is to say
(I'm moderating now, I'm reasonable—compromise) the name
of the brand, just mention the name, just to remind everybody
that the despicable cancer kings are after their coin, and that's
it. No groovy tastes, no super sex scenes, no obscene comparisons
to springtime which if anything is holy is and must be kept so.
Period. Got it? Okay. I expect to have it done or I'll just be really
mad and I don't know what I'll do, I don't know, but I'll take
care of business in some way so as to make things a little more
right.

Three days, one hour, eighteen minutes, and you've got me
again, bastards. I'm in Marlboro country.

Now about that meeting with Bercaw.
He was saying that the administration man he was work-
ing with was "a Kirk tool, or flunky, or whatever."
"The hearings are a big show. We couldn't get money or
stationery. Big sham.
"We want to get them to make a statement recognizing the
Revolution. Temple kept trying to avoid discussing issues 'be-

yond the mandate of the Committee.' He's only concerned with restructuring.

"Such bullshit. And they're getting away with it too, because they control everything. If they ever say they considered student views, we could call it a lie and resign as a group. But now I think it might be good to play along for a while.

"We've got a problem. There are no radicals on the Committee. The jocks think *we're* radical and they're moderate. You see what we're going through? It's crazy. To one side everybody's a Commie, to the other everybody's CIA.

"I feel incompetent. I don't know what's going on. Rudd called me a liberal. Students for a Restructured University called me reactionary. It's crazy."

He was talking faster and faster and laughing sporadically. He wanted very badly for me to tell him he wasn't incompetent. I didn't. He is incompetent. Everybody is. I asked him what role he played in the strike.

"I was so far out of it," he reminisced. "I thought it was a big unnecessary noise. I was like a trustee. Since then I've been radicalized. A lot of it's bullshit but a lot of it's true."

His mood changed as something crossed his mind. "Rudd's tried to use me already, the bastard. I'll get thrown out of here, too.

"A cute little thing you might add—" he said. "I held the Trustees captive for about thirty seconds. We were going to take Low Library and turn it into an old-age home for retired millionaires—only way to make them listen."

He elaborated on the function Barnard girls would fulfill in this establishment.

Back to reality he pointed out that the Trustees refused to have a stenographer sit in on the meetings, and there was water in glasses for the Trustees, but not for the student representatives. He felt that was symbolic.

Vice-President Truman had said he didn't know where he could get money for the student representatives.

"I said sell a building," Bercaw recalled. "You've got to tell these guys."

He told me about a representative from the art school whom everybody thought was a radical because of his sideburns, and then he told me all about Rudd.

"The news media made him what he is. He's a symbol. I think he's a very bright person and he's got *chutzpa*. A charming person, a sharp boy, but not the driving force behind the strike."

"Who was the driving force?" I asked.

"I don't know," he said. He got militant to make up for that. "If we don't get what we want, I'm all for doing it again, except stronger," he asserted.

I asked him if he'd be willing to get arrested.

"I don't know if I'd go that far," he reasoned. "I've never participated in a demonstration. There are specialists these days, right? That's SDS's specialty. That's their thing. Want some more tea?"

I took some and he continued.

"The Trustees are like the board of directors of any other corporation. *Other* corporation. Say that I said *other*. Say it's significant."

It's significant.

"The Trustees think that the Students for a Restructured University—the liberals—are a bunch of Communists. Isn't it incredible?

"I've been incredibly enlightened over the past three months. If that's the only way you can do it, politicize, we gotta have a strike every year.

"The Trustees are scared shit. They're definitely concerned. Because they don't have control of the situation. They're still playing the game that SDS is not a legitimate group. I think they still think of students as an unnecessary entity."

Bercaw liked to talk, but I liked to listen. I would go so far as to say that I liked Bercaw. Bercaw—misrepresenting student views on a crisis he had no part in to a group of men who don't listen anyway. What a guy.

"We submitted an agenda to the Executive Director of the Committee. He wrote back saying why they couldn't use it." He showed me the letter.

"I should have underlined things in it," he said. "There are real turd things in that letter."

He showed me a letter from Trustee Charles Luce. I almost dropped it in awe. The letterhead read, "Chairman of the Board, Consolidated Edison Co." It was like holding the Dead Sea Scrolls.

"I know," said Bercaw. "All that guy has to do is raise his finger and ten billion dollars goes flying off in some direction. But you rap to him like anybody else. You know he was once almost kicked out of Wisconsin State over freedom of the college press?

"They, the administration and Trustees"—this was his summation—"they made us, they created us, they put our picture in *The Times*; now they can't come out and say we're not a legitimate group."

(Most students said that about the Temple Committee representatives from the start.)

"You know?" he said. "The alumni think Grayson Kirk is saving the University from Communists."

We agreed that Grayson Kirk had been a tremendous boon to the radical movement; he swore several times that he would denounce the Trustees if things came to that; and we shook hands, as one usually does when one leaves, which I did.

I now took a cab to Laura's. I've taken hundreds of cabs to Laura's. I asked the cab driver if he'd heard of Mark Rudd. He had. I asked what he thought of him. I asked it loudly as he said he didn't hear very well. He was somewhat older than most people are.

"I'm sure Mark Rudd knows more about what he's doing than I do," he said.

I wondered how he reacted to him on T.V.

"It seemed like he was dedicated to what he was striving for.

He seemed to be fighting for what he thought was right."

He asked me if we'd won anything. I said the gym is stopped, but the war research will probably go on as usual. I said there'll be more trouble in the fall.

"I hope some compromise can be worked out to the complete satisfaction of the students, because that's better than fighting," he said.

This man, by the stickers in the cab windows, had contributed some money to everything. He began to talk about politicians.

"Politicians need a little prodding to show them that if they don't do what's right, come next semester they won't be in the class, as they say in school parlance."

My ego smashed through the flimsy walls of my character and told him I was writing. He encouraged me to write. He said writers open up a whole new world to people. He liked reading magazines and newspapers, and even the dictionary. He likes to read the dictionary to pick up words.

He talked about cops. He talked about how when a woman he knows was robbed in the subway, there was no cop around. He prefaced his remarks by saying, "Let's assume that cops are regular guys trying to do the best they can." I said "Okay, just for the sake of argument." Yet he'd just read about a man who was given a summons by a cop for taking a newspaper out of a trash can. ("He wasn't going to throw it on the floor. He was going to read it. Here was a man who was happy at the thought of having saved himself ten cents and that he was going to have something to read that night.") He also didn't like the way cops demand free rides from him, or the way they manage to get their groceries free. He also didn't like Mayor Lindsay appointing people to jobs and then raising their salaries by $15,000 right away. "The unfairness of it just rankles you. But who am I to fight City Hall? I'm not strong enough." But he believed that things have a way of working out for the best with a little help from people, and he believed in the importance of believing that.

We ultimately arrived and he said "Well, I hope everything

works out well for me, for the young people, for the country, for Biafra."

I gave that man such a big tip like you wouldn't believe.
After visiting with Laura, I went to the Strategy Meeting.

THE STRATEGY MEETING

I was an hour and a half late to the strategy meeting. I wanted to be. Strategy meetings last an awfully long time. When I got there, there were so many people in the room that it was so hot that I left. But I stood at the window.

A guy was giving a well-researched report on "urban removal" plans. They had a petition to circulate urging that instead of the city buying sites and selling them to institutions, the city should confiscate already bought sites from the institutions.

I went inside and saw leftist Biggee Lew Cole, whom I don't trust any more. He had just got back from Bermuda and he looked tanned and healthy, and revolutionaries are supposed to be wan.

A girl had two dogs with her. They were quiet, but still we didn't need two dogs.

Then there was a debate between Papert for the Labor Committee and Rudd and a Gilbert for the action faction.

"Between the farmer and the consumer there are a lot of phony capitalist forms," Papert pointed out, for some reason. Then he went into a little SDS history.

At one point he had wanted a gym demonstration, but some of SDS fought it, calling it paternalistic, saying if students demonstrate there, then it will imply it's Columbia property. "Perhaps that implies," he said, "that we students are Columbia property."

"What will kill the strike," he emphasized, "is if we confine it to student issues. We have to broaden the issues involved and the people involved."

Rudd got up and said that he agreed with the first part of what Papert said, "I mean everybody wants the Revolution."

Then he yielded to his economist friend who rapped on about "the social disequilibrium of the market system," and maldistribution of wealth and how this leads to "imperialism abroad and a forced consumption culture at home. These are all connected with the central dynamics of capitalism."

He said that the majority of the people in America are oppressed. He talked about different strata of workers and how white workers may see their interests as against those of black workers.

(Sometimes when I hear white and black I think of the Queen of Hearts' chess game or color war at summer camp or war games but never anything real. Do you realize how ridiculous it sounds? The whites versus the blacks? Come on.)

"The defining characteristic of production in America is anti-social," he concluded, pointing to increased wild-cat strikes as evidence of growing rejection of the system.

Rudd talked again.

"We can't aim broadsides at the working class," he said. "We have to focus on groups, for example—hospital workers. Why are they an underclass? What is the reason for the class nature of hospital service?"

He also said that the legal system is an out and out means of control. He also said that Columbia can pay workers' economic demands. "What must be exposed is its middle-class elitism." And he also said that "We can't create a free or socialist university in an unfree society. We have to have a Revolution."

The man to the right of me had three dials on his watch and was jiggling his knee. The boy to my left finished all the orange juice that was being passed around when he got it, and the girl on my left kept talking all the time. Such are the things that bother me a lot, especially in hot crowded places.

Mr. Papert spoke once more.

"The inflated rents around here are not based on the value of the garbage property. They're based on the speculative value of the titles to the garbage property.

"Mark goes around yelling 'Patch up the ceiling,' but that

would make him a reformist, so he says 'Patch up the ceiling, Revolution!' and he thinks that will make people revolutionaries."

A graduate student put in that he felt the question was "whether you're going to say lower the subway fare five cents or go around explaining why it's too high. We shouldn't be pushed to say exactly what we want and why, because that's necessarily reformist."

He added that the capitalist crisis is not falling rates of profits, but underconsumption. (I know *I'm* not underconsuming.)

The next to speak was a very erudite and aged-looking fellow with a beard and everything. He said that "Some say that FDR's New Deal fundamentally changed the nature of capitalism with built-in stabilizers so there will never be a crisis in the advanced capitalist nations again. But if the banks had stayed open two more days in the gold crisis, we'd all have been in the midst of a world depression. If you subscribe to the underconsumption theory"—(the only thing I subscribe to is *Modern Photography*. I had no idea what he was talking about, but his intonation was lively and I listened attentively)—"there is no crisis. But there *is* a crisis.

"The history of revolutionary processes is one of abrupt changes brought by economic crises. . . . The system is turning to the club. In exact proportion to how much Johnson is unwilling to buy the blacks off, he talks about crime in the streets."

I went out for some ice tea. Sometimes in the summer in the City I feel like some British Foreign Office cat holding on in India. I live from one iced drink to the next.

I met a friend on the sidewalk. He told me about how a Barnard girl is busy plagiarizing my articles for a screenplay she's writing.

"You'll have to sue," he said.

"I know," I agreed, "but that would be awfully crass."

"You could kill her," he suggested.

I thought that was a terrific idea. It would fit in much better with the revolutionary scene than bourgeois court proceedings would.

"I'll wipe her out," I decided. "You see, I've been acclimated or adjusted to being bought off, and I expect to continue being bought off."

"It's much better than being sold out," he agreed. "I hear you're making oodles of money."

"Yeah. But I never see any of it. It's all in the future. At some point we'll converge, me and the money."

"So is that what you're doing this summer, converging with your money?"

"Yeah," I supposed so. "I'm moving inexorably through time, trying to catch up with my coin."

I watered myself and returned to the meeting.

Jones was saying that the gritty is not some depression in '58 but Nam, oppression, and young people on the move. He told a tale about a Communist Party cell in Chicago that had eight students and a worker. The worker took acid and the students threw him out.

This somehow inspired the resident trade unionist to speak.

"Workers are neither reactionary nor progressive," he said, "but potentially revolutionary. But if you think you can go in and tell the workers what to do, you're badly mistaken. They'll consider you alien and pompous. If you're serious about winning the workers, go work in the shops."

J.J. now wanted to speak and did.

"The proletariat of American capitalism is the international proletariat of the third world."

J.J.'s real name is John Jacobs and with his beard and hair he looks a lot like Jesus.

"People make a big deal of the death of Che in the mountains at the age of thirty-nine," he continued. "What they don't appreciate is that thirty-nine is the life expectancy in the third world.

"Youth doesn't have the vested interest in stability that any worker with a steady job has. Parents in the home are socializing agents for the consumer society. Thus the youth revolt is a spontaneous manifestation of the class struggle." This was his theory of "proletarianized youth."

Fat Eric (as he is called) spoke next, briefly. "I have heard tonight economic analysis from all sides that can be characterized by one word—bullshit." This brought thunderous and sustained applause.

A woman teacher, who hangs around fulfilling everyone's mother need, spoke ominously for a moment. "To be against the system is not enough. Mussolini came from the left that way. Hitting the streets is not enough."

This did not sit well with everyone. Then something percolated from a perky little Barnard girl. "Everything I've heard tonight is either esoteric or nasty. [Cartoonist Thomas Nast used to be mean.] What was great about the strike was that we thought a little less and felt a little more." She added that she was not against thinking.

In wrapping up, Papert said that "J.J. is for a minority Revolution, whereas Gilbert doesn't like violence that much and wants to have more people on his side. The groups in motion are not the revolutionary agent; the agent is yet to be created."

And J.J. said, "I don't see a Revolution coming now in this country," which surprised me greatly because he's the shoot-'em-up character of the Columbia left.

It being then the next morning already and still hot out, the meeting ended.

I went for food with Mark Rudd.

MARK RUDD

Mark Rudd, President Columbia SDS, Public Figure, idol to the boppers of the nation, has neither horns nor rays of light emanating from his brow. He could be the boy next door, if he happened to live there.

He said that that woman had come within a hair of accusing us of proto-fascism, which is something he hears quite frequently.

I asked him what he felt about the number of paranoids and raving loonies in the movement.

"SDS has probably less neurotics than most groups of people," he said. "At least the actions we take aren't manifestations of neurosis."

I wondered if he recognized any mistakes he'd made.

"We made about fifty the first day," he said, "but it worked out okay."

"We shouldn't have given power to a coalition Strike Committee. We should have retained power for the communes.

"A personal mistake was allowing myself to become the symbol of the strike."

With regard to leaving Hamilton that first Wednesday morning, he said "We had to leave Hamilton. The blacks are so into their own thing. We needed the trauma of leaving to learn the importance of militance, of staying."

Could we have left the buildings if the administration had condescended to negotiate and granted something?

"The administration was so stupid," he said, his face showing amazement still in remembering. "But I wouldn't have left til we won all our demands."

I asked him honestly if he knew anything. I mean, did he know economics or sociology or anything. Actually I just wanted to know what he's got that anybody doesn't have.

He said he knew history, and he said that he had a sense of what the Movement is, and a basic optimism.

Is there anything he wouldn't do to build the Revolution, like would he slash Kirk's Rembrandt if he thought it would help?

"There's nothing I wouldn't do," he said.

Is there really going to be a Revolution? (That's what I want to know. What is games and what is real?)

He said there certainly would be, but not in eighteen months, as some of the Labor Committee people are fond of saying.

I read him Dan's account of the Harlem march, and asked him if it was accurate, or did he always know precisely what he was doing.

"It was clear that it was good to have people in the streets," he said. "When liberals chant 'Ho Ho Ho,' it's good . . . I had apprehensions about whether to go to Harlem. I changed my mind three times. People are allowed to change their minds. It wasn't important either way, whether we smashed windows."

"Are you enjoying your life?" I had asked him once, and he had said no, he felt imprisoned by some things. Now I asked him what things.

He said that he'd had a cold and trouble with his girl on the day I asked him; in fact, he rather thought he was enjoying his life. But he did feel imprisoned by his too many responsibilities. He said he'd like to get away.

Just to round out his character sketch, I asked him if he smoked.

"I'm not going to tell you," he said.

"No, cigarettes, I mean," I explained.

"Oh. No, I don't," he said.

He very rarely drinks.

Thursday, August 1: I worked on the Book Thursday, August first. I called Tony Papert to apologize for not showing up at his apartment the night before, and found out he has a cold. He has a cold, I have a cold, Rudd has a cold, Laura has a cold. Everybody has a cold.

In the nighttime, at 9 P.M. to be exact, for those craving exactness, I went to Laura's, which would not be unusual but for what we saw on T.V. there. We saw the Yankees beat the Red Sox, but that isn't what I want to bring to your attention. The thing is that we saw the Les Crane show, and on the Les Crane show were the founder of the W.E.B. Dubois Clubs and a former member of a Dubois Club.

The former member had for two years worked as an undercover agent for the Chicago police, infiltrating the Dubois Club in San Francisco. He was with the Red Squad of the police, and all the while he was a member of the John Birch Society. He had discovered, to his and the House Un-American Activities

Committee's satisfaction, that Communists were behind the urban ghetto riots. He supported the HUAC's Luce Report, which recommended issuing I.D. cards to blacks and shipping suspicious individuals to detention camps. He agreed with J. Edgar Hoover's statement that Martin Luther King was "the most notorious liar in America." He was a backward and hateful man, and he was in the employ of the police.

So, there are secret police. There are red squads. There are agents and provocateurs. There are. I know that. It makes me sick. You know that, too.

Friday, August 2: Evening. The breeze blows on me. I can feel every molecule brush by—no, it is the rustling of my hairs. I see endless huge plains of tall waving grass in Africa. The wind(ow) screaming as it cuts through, bending, but not breaking, the grass.

Then, the sound of a plane, an old plane, over the fields. A tiger crouches under the sound! But wait, it is a biplane in W.W. I. It's a dogfight. Guns, smoke, whirling in air. But then back to Africa.

Where the leaping antelope just barely brush the grass seeds on top, as they fly in graceful terror from the sound of man.

Went with Laura to see *The Green Berets*, the late showing, in Times Square. That flick can really blow your high, as the saying goes. We walked in early and saw the ending first, which heightened the suspense.

People in the audience applauded the killing, but not to any great extent. They just thought it was cool, a judgment completely independent of any political or moral consideration.

Still, it was a very depressing experience. The movie was essentially made by the government. And it is bad. Somehow, it's saddening to see the government be such a failure even at being evil. I felt it would have been better if they had made their propaganda with some finesse, some craft. But the thing is so lousy in every way. It's boring. There's nothing worse than boring evil, unless it's boring evil featuring an obese John Wayne.

· · ·

The Kid yawned.

"I yawned," said the Kid. "I don't mind admitting it. Napoleon yawned, Joan of Arc yawned, Che yawned, Dubcek yawns. I yawn."

Saturday, August 3: Laura and I, out of a sense of duty, went to what we correctly knew would be a very boring peace demonstration in Times Square. Peace demonstrations as a genre are very boring, and if you've got a very boring example of one, then you've got sort of boring *squared* and, well, that just doesn't make it.

Nonetheless, things, as is their wont, happened.

I experienced a little reinforcement learning regarding *guanos* (worms—right-wing Cubans). I was standing there in the police barricade demo playpen, reading a flyer about *guanos* and how they go around bombing leftist establishments and being generally obnoxious and how the police afford us no protection, when suddenly about five fiery little Latin Fascists jumped into the crowd beside me and started punching people.

I am not privy to the secrets of my mind, but for some reason at this particular juncture I was not afraid and jumped into the fray. But you know how frays are. I couldn't tell who was who, what with all the straight-looking liberals at the demonstration, and the cops complicated things by clubbing everybody without regard to politics or national origin.

All this lasted about forty-five seconds, but before it was over I found a worm making off with a Youth Against War and Fascism flag. I grabbed it and pulled it away from him, which wasn't hard, because I don't think he wanted it much more than I did.

The only other unpleasant worm action of the afternoon was that they let off four or five canisters of tear gas a few blocks away. New York air doesn't need tear gas.

After the endless speeches ended, we walked to a nearby

National Guard armory "to talk with the soldiers," an unrealistic proposal on two counts. First of all, any troops in the vicinity would not be made available for conversation, and second, National Guardsmen are a long way from being soldiers.

Before we marched off I shook hands with a rookie cop whose eyes had previously caught my eyes and Laura's too. He had tipped his cap and smiled at us. I told him not to get taken for the TPF, and he asked me if he could have my YAWF flag. I gave it to him. That man was not a pig.

Some cops are. Most people agree that there are good cops and bad. But everybody assumes that there have to be cops, that there always have been. I have no plan for abolishing police forces, but I do think people should consider that police are not the most natural thing in the world, not even one of the more natural things. It seems strange to me that a few men should be taken from the community and given the job of watching out for it. A cop is a man who goes home and takes off his blues and goes to bed with his wife or maybe fights with her. Yet if he tells me to move, I'm supposed to move. Maybe I don't want to move. Maybe I want *him* to move. But he's got his club and his gun and everybody seems to think that's the way it's supposed to be. I don't know. I think about it sometimes.

On the way to the Guard place an old woman suggested that I "go back to Russia." I answered, essentially, that I live here, that I couldn't, after five years of study, speak hardly any Russian, that the winters there are too severe, and that, anyway, my grandparents had come here *from* there, so what did she want, some sort of shuttle?

We got to the armory and marched around the walls several times, but no one had a trumpet.

That night Laura and I went to a place called Friar Tuck's for dinner. It cost a good sum of the old coin, and we were concerned about it being kind of anti-revolutionary to dine out. That actually bothered us a bit.

There are many problems that come with the new left thing.

.   .   .

Sunday, August 4: I visited Mrs. Hotzelove across the hall. She made me a highball and we talked.

She was against long hair. "If men wear it long, women should wear it short." And beards. "I see a boy with a beard. He's clean —I believe he's clean—but he doesn't look it.

"I love young people, all of them. What would we do without them? But they have crazy ways to dress."

She's seventy-five and in New York since 1908.

"Fifty years ago young people were calmer like. But every generation has some crazy dance. So they have crazy dances now, too. They should have more polkas.

"One thing I don't approve of young people is the Columbia thing. They're there to learn. That was sad things. So much damage. Such a school like Columbia."

I told her that I'm from Columbia.

"I don't mean they should kick you out," she explained, "but they should give you a good scolding.

"I like young people, even if they're crazy," she reaffirmed. "What am I going to do? I like them."

Vietnam came up, as it must in any conversation in America.

"I'm against the war," she said, "because wars never win anything. But what am I going to do?"

She's from Czechoslovakia and she talked about that. "Again war. I wouldn't be surprised if there was something."

But she said she was principally concerned with America which is her country. She came here because she "didn't have enough to eat on the other side. I never had to worry about being hungry here because I worked."

That last was a pointed remark.

"This new generation thinks they should get something for nothing." She mentioned for example a young man who hangs around our building, living off his mother. "I would support him," she said, "I'd support him with a stick on the head."

Taking all of this into account, I wondered who she'd vote for this fall.

"Wallace—that's out," she said. "He's too much against the

colored people. Rockefeller's too rich. Nixon—he's running all the time. I don't care for Humphrey."

She's for McCarthy, but not especially, because she's sure he won't be nominated. She liked Roosevelt very much because "he was for poor people. Young people going to get old some time. With social security at least you don't feel like a beggar altogether."

I liked Mrs. Hotzelove very much. It's too bad the landlord is throwing her out, after thirty years, to renovate the apartment.

I went to my room and decided to call a Trustee, more for a goof.

I called Luce and had my number taken. I called Petersen and spoke to his son as sweat streamed down my face. It was hot. He told me to try again at 9:45 that evening.

There was no answer at Kappel's. I was glad. What if there was an answer?

I thought I might try Buttenweiser next, because I've heard he likes to talk, and he's a McCarthy delegate which—although it worries me about The Clean One—at least meant we'd have a common ground. But I wasn't sure how to pronounce his name.

I tried Temple. A foreign-accented woman, possibly his grandmother, but more likely his maid, said he was on vacation at Martha's Vineyard. I wondered if Bercaw knew that.

I tried Hogan—no answer.

I began to dial them all. Seeing that I wouldn't get to talk to any of them, there was nothing to fear.

At 9:45 exactly I called Petersen. It seemed that he had come in and gone out again, and would not be back until late.

Monday, August 5: I decided to zero in on Chairman of the Board Petersen, he being the ace top Biggee. I called him at the Irving Trust Co.

I actually spoke to him, or someone who purported to be him. It occurred to me that I had no way of knowing whether it was actually Petersen. I asked him what the Trustees were doing to avoid a blow-up in the fall.

"It's the administration that maintains law and order," he said.

Beyond that he would not answer my questions, but commented on my asking them.

"When history is written up too currently," he commented, "there are pros and cons regarding its merits."

That there are.

I called Hogan (Trustee-District Attorney Man) to be told by one operator that he was on another line, and by a second that he was on vacation. Perhaps in some sense they were both right. I don't know, but I don't care.

In the afternoon I finally took up Archibald Cox's suggestion that I come in and look over the testimony given his Commission. There were 3534 pages of it.

I looked up the day Dean Platt testified, July 15, shortly before he resigned. He was talking about the events of May 21, when Rudd and four others refused to come into the Dean's office.

"I was well aware they had no intention of coming in," Dean Platt said.

Cox: "So this [calling them in] was all, in a sense, a charade, so far as you could see?"

"Well, as best—my prediction at the time was they would not come in," Platt replied. "The five students were never formally informed that they could stand mute."

Regarding the twenty-eight seniors who subsequently obeyed a call to see the Dean, Platt said, "Of the fifteen students who pleaded guilty by standing mute, eight—"

Cox interrupted: "Pleaded guilty by standing mute?"

Platt: "I'm sorry. Correction. Pleaded not guilty by standing mute. . . .

"A student who pleaded guilty immediately qualified for the degree."

"It has sort of an odd flavor to it, doesn't it," said Professor Cox.

"Yes, it does," agreed Dean Platt.

Returning to the subject of the Rudd five, Dean Platt said, "My surmise is that if they pleaded guilty, I would make the decision of suspension, and that in spite of recommendations of the Joint Disciplinary Committee that no action be taken until the resolution of the criminal charges, that they would be suspended immediately.

"My surmise is that if they stood mute or pleaded not guilty, they would go immediately to a college tribunal which would just make a decision of guilty and that they would be suspended immediately."

Professor Cox asked if Dean Platt was free to decide perhaps not to suspend them.

The answer was no.

The five's lawyers had asked for a day's extension. Was Platt "free to grant that request?"

No.

The Columbia discipline system ought to merge with the Penn Central.

In the evening I went to court over my parking tickets, particularly the one for illegal parking in a place that had no sign declaring its out-of-bounds status.

The Strike Legal Committee stresses that the courts serve the Propertied. That wouldn't surprise me, so since I don't own any means of production, I came armed to the teeth with two double-weight glossy 8x10 black and white photographs to bolster my case.

There were over one hundred people in the courtroom and I had to wait. The woman beside me saw a man she knew and said "Meter." "How are the kids?" he replied.

People passed before the judge at the rate of three per minute. Cosmo, Anastasia, Woodrow . . . the names were called. People have a wide variety of names.

A fat woman and her fat daughter were charged with double parking, which struck me as funny. A woman stood before the bench nearly weeping.

"You're a nice lady," the judge said. "No fine." That set the crowd buzzing. "Can I borrow her next?" the man beside me said.

It turned out that I had once more failed to fathom the intricacies of the American judicial process. In this court you plead guilty and have your fine reduced to thank you for coming. For the not-guilty photo case I have to return next April.

The judge looked exactly like Grayson Kirk, except with no worry in his face.

That night I listened to WABC for one solid hour, to check out what *Forbes* magazine calls "The Record Business/Psychedelic Billions." (In their July 15 issue *Forbes* advised, "Don't call it noise, dad. Try to dig it. For it's really the sound of music, today's and tomorrow's, and, what's more, it's the sound of money, maybe $2 billion worth.")

I heard the station identified seventeen times. Six times I heard the jingle "Charlie Greer—music Pow! Pow! Power!" Seven minutes I spent listening to poetry extolling Denison's Clothiers in New Jersey. "Folks, the cat in the bag will never do/We need you and your money, too/We'll even take your money without you/Just bring money/Money talks/Nobody walks."

And the D.J. told one joke. "I used to go with a girl who used to be called the belle of the ball. One night they rang her neck."

Thankfully I went to bed.

Tuesday, August 6: I flew home to work on the Book. This was no mean trick, since the craft was considerably heavier than air, and the weather was, well, it was like this:

You've got an albino goldfish, right? And it's blind. Okay. You take your bowl of milk and you put your goldfish in it. The blind albino one. So it wouldn't be able to see it's own nose, right? Well, that's what the weather was like.

Here, arbitrarily, the Book ends.

Postscript

SEX

The sexual revolution is like most other things: it may or may not exist. If it does exist, it may be good or bad but will probably avail itself of the opportunity to be both. One thing is certain: sex is running rampant, unchecked, and spreading like wildfire.

I am inclined to believe that this is pretty much as it has always been, but since I really know neither how it has always been nor how it is now, I am not especially qualified to make judgment. If pressed, however, I would probably say that there are indeed sexually revolutionary cadres, whose principal effect is to depress the hell out of everybody who is not in one.

What is perhaps significant is that the feeling of the outs for the ins is primarily one of jealousy, coupled with admiration or, on bad days, hatred; never moral indignation. With regard to hyperactive girls, the terms harlot, bawd, strumpet, street walker, call girl, B-girl, prostitute, fille de joie, evildoer, sinner, transgressor, profligate, libertine, fallen angel, courtesan, doxy,

wanton, tart, chippy, wench, trollop, light-o'-love, or whore
are seldom, if ever, used and nymphomaniac only occasionally.
And the last is a morally neutral term.

At Columbia the administration recently liberalized women's
dorm regulations. They could have abolished them altogether,
either the restrictions or the privileges, with equal effect on most
residents. The consensus was that liberal rules are a nice thing
to have around just in case the situation ever arises.

As to whether the new rules, allowing cohabitation for a few
hours every day of the week, are really liberal—yes, they are.
Liberal is exactly what they are. They sound progressive but
entirely skirt the basic issue: whether the University should have
any say over its students' personal lives.

Also at Columbia was the Linda-Peter case, which splashed all
over the newspapers of the entire country. The two, unmarried,
lived in conjugation with each other and a mimeograph machine
in an off-campus apartment, and had the temerity to give an
anonymous interview to *The New York Times*. The interview
did not remain anonymous however. The forces of righteousness
and remote birth dates rallied at Barnard to crush the offender,
who didn't seem to overly care, which was to her credit, although
she couldn't resist cranking out a few mimeos about herself,
which was not.

In college, everything is to be done with discretion. Except at
fraternities, which are themselves out—drunken orgies are out
—as are Wesson Oil parties and statutory rape. It is in to love a
person and express it however you want. However, nothing is
in or *out*, so all such distinctions are entirely spurious except for
journalistic purposes.

DRUGS

There certainly are.

You've got your nicotine and alcohol and caffeine, and there's
marijuana, hash, peyote, and LSD and STP and DMT and
THC, and you've got your meta-amphetamine-hydrochloride.
There are those who smoke opium, and then there are the drug-

store drugs: Dexedrine (the No-Doz of the collegiate world), Seconal, Dexamyl, phenobarbital, Darvon, Escatrol, codeine, paregoric, you know.

Grass is a little less common than cigarettes. When someone says "stoned," he doesn't mean drunk. Heroin is avoided.

A friend of mine goes on at length about "choir-like erasma-tites" and "hard and heated ice" and "pillowed wonders of ground hogs"—all the usual things. Let's just say that if you smoke and drink at the same time, you're after your head.

VIOLENCE

So long as it is considered acceptable for the government to kill hundreds of thousands for no reason at all, individuals will consider it all right to kill just one person whom they hate very much for what they consider to be a very good reason.

The *Boston Globe* editorialized: "No one needs to be reminded again of the three most terrible killings of the past five years." There were 12,000 homicides last year, but apparently they weren't that bad; they weren't as terrible as the most terrible, at least.

I don't know if Americans are sick, but I would go so far as to say that I heard a button vender, outside a funeral in New York, yelling "Remember Bobby—fifty cents."

Explanatory Note

This is what the Book has been about.

At Columbia University in the City of New York, in the spring of 1968, there was an uprising of students against the administration of their school.

Columbia is an Ivy League school. Ivy League schools are known for good scholarship and poor football teams, a situation which shows signs of reversing. They are also known for being stodgily proper, populated by nice people.

It came as a shock, then, to everyone, that the administration of an Ivy League school should be so un-nice as to involve their institution in racism and war, and that the students should be so ill-mannered as to do something about it.

These developments were fascinating to the populace at large, to many of whom Columbia had meant some place where Juan Valdez eked out a miserable pittance delivering coffee beans to El Exigente. The trouble on campus made good video entertainment and sold many newspapers, firmly establishing itself in event reality.

I can assure you that the Columbia action cannot be dismissed as an overgrown panty raid, a manifestation of the vernal urge. It lasted too long; participants endured hardships, and worse, boredom, conditions through which collegiate fetishistic folly could never sustain itself.

Beyond defining what it wasn't, it is very difficult to say with certainty what anything meant. But everything must have a meaning, and everyone is free to say what meanings are.

At Columbia a lot of students simply did not like their school commandeering a park and they rather disapproved of their school making war, and they told other students who told others and we saw that Columbia is our school and we will have something to say for what it does.

I declare that the meaning of the Columbia uprising is that one too many persons has been educated, and one too many wires has linked people's thoughts together, for power to breed power any more.

Afterword

There are those who want an armed Revolution and I am not one of them. Not just now. But I do have a statement to make at this time, gentlemen.

Since the First Republic of the United States is one hundred ninety-two years old and I am nineteen, I will give it one more chance.

But if the Democrats do not nominate Clean, whom against my better judgment I love, or if they do nominate Clean and he turns out to be what I suspect but won't admit he is, then I will have no recourse but to acknowledge that democracy is not only dead, but is also not about to be revived through democratic means.

I do not want to fight in Vietnam, of course. But I also don't want to have to fight the draft, or fight the law, or fight anything. I'm a nineteen-year-old civilian, and I am tired of fighting.

One of these days I may fight in earnest and altogether so that I won't have to fight any more.

ABOUT THE AUTHOR

JAMES SIMON KUNEN was a Columbia College sophmore when he wrote *The Strawberry Statement*. After his graduation from Columbia, his reporting from Vietnam for *TRUE* magazine led to his second book, *Standard Operating Procedure* (1971). Subsequently, as a conscientious objector, Kunen worked as a counselor at a group home for youthful offenders in Lancaster, Mass. He graduated from New York University Law School, became a public defender in the criminal courts of Washington, D.C., and recounted his experiences in *"How Can You Defend Those People?"* (1983). He left the practice of law, returned to journalism, and has written for *The New Yorker, People, Newsday, The New York Times Magazine* and many other publications. His fourth book, *Reckless Disregard*, an exposé of Ford Motor Company's role in a 27-fatality school bus fire, was published by Simon & Schuster in 1994. Kunen is married to radio journalist Lisa Karlin; they live with their two children in Brooklyn, N.Y.

CPSIA information can be obtained
at www.ICGtesting.com
Printed in the USA
LVOW03s0954210817

545784LV00004B/519/P

9 781881 089520